How To...
Play Boogie Woogie Piano

BY ARTHUR MIGLIAZZA AND DAVE RUBIN

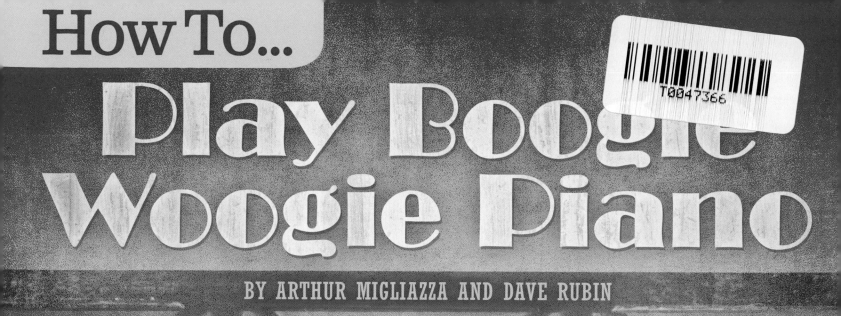

To access audio visit:
www.halleonard.com/mylibrary

Enter Code
3768-9912-1643-1970

HAL•LEONARD®
7777 W. BLUEMOUND RD. P.O. BOX 13819 MILWAUKEE, WI 53213

In Australia Contact:
Hal Leonard Australia Pty. Ltd.
4 Lentara Court
Cheltenham, Victoria, 3192 Australia
Email: ausadmin@halleonard.com.au

Visit Hal Leonard Online at
www.halleonard.com

This book is dedicated to you, the student. It was written in the spirit of passing on what so many before have known and accomplished. You are the future of this music, and your studies ensure that it will not be forgotten.

CONTENTS

INTRODUCTION

Of the handful of professional boogie woogie piano players in the world, even fewer teach. Every step I take with a student builds upon what came before. I believe that such an approach, by someone who plays the style authentically, has never before existed. It has been 17 years in the making and now I have it almost down to a science. I have had the incredible fortune to learn from some of the best players of the boogie woogie style, including Ann Rabson, Mr. B, Henry Butler, and Bob Seeley, among others. All were incredibly generous with their knowledge.

In addition, I have had the good fortune to teach alongside Ann Rabson, Daryl Davis, Chase Garrett, Erwin Helfer, and many other contemporary boogie woogie players. When it comes to playing boogie woogie and blues piano styles, I follow a systematic and logical approach to teaching. I can take a dedicated student who knows nothing of piano, let alone boogie woogie, and teach them how to become their own teacher.

—Arthur Migliazza

THE HISTORY OF BOOGIE WOOGIE PIANO

Though parts of Beethoven's *Piano Sonata No. 32 in C Minor, Op. 111* (1821-22) sound to modern ears remarkably like 20th-century stride and even boogie woogie music, the generally accepted roots go back to the late 19th century African-American community. The development of the genre is inextricably intertwined with that of the shuffle rhythm as the powerful walking and moving bass lines provided the driving, swinging propulsion. Serious research into the origins of the style did not occur until the 1930s with the collection of oral histories. According to the noted African-American author, folklorist, and anthropologist Nora Zeale Hurston (1891-1960), the groundwork for the style was originally laid by guitarists as entertainment, likely beginning in rough work camps in northeast Texas in the 1870s:

One guitar was enough for a dance. To have two was considered excellent. Where two were playing, one man played the lead and the other seconded him. The first player was "picking" and the second was "framming," that is, playing chords while the lead carried the melody by dexterous finger work. Sometimes a third player was added, and he played a tom-tom effect on the lower strings.

Dr. John Tennison, a renowned researcher into the origins of boogie woogie, in 2010 identified Marshall, Texas in the northeast "Piney Woods" of Harrison County as Ground Zero for the music from 1870-80. Since 2011, the town has proudly called itself "The Birthplace of Boogie Woogie."

As the 19th century wore on, pianos took the place of guitars in lumber, mining, railroad, and turpentine camps in the Midwest and South. Though it is conjecture, the practicality of employing one musician versus two or three – plus the sheer increase in volume afforded by pianos instead of acoustic guitars in noisy, rowdy barrelhouses – makes sense of the change. There is less ambiguity, however, about the music performed. Quite simply, patrons wanted to hear the same raucous, rolling rhythms, so piano players devised left-hand patterns analogous to rhythm guitar parts while embellishing and soloing with the right hand.

In time, "walking bass lines" derived from the major scale or the Mixolydian mode appeared. In reference, the late great Eubie Blake described the early proto-boogie piano playing of 300-pound William Turk:

He had a left hand like God. He didn't even know what key he was playing in, but he played them all. He would play the ragtime stride bass, but it bothered him because his stomach got in the way of his arm, so he used a walking bass instead. I can remember when I was 13 – this was in 1896 – how Turk would play one note with his right hand and at the same time four with his left. We called it "sixteen" and they call it boogie woogie now.

The "sixteen" Blake mentioned could be seen as the number of notes played in typical two-measure walking-bass line patterns with eight notes ascending and eight descending in pairs. In addition, boogie woogie was called "fast Western" or "fast Texas" in reference to the Texas Western Railroad Company of Harrison County. The connection between trains and blues/ boogie woogie is immediately clear in the clickety-clack rhythms of the latter, for example. Furthermore, according to blues scholar Tom Fleming, "During slavery the attraction to the railroad was both real and symbolic. Southern railroads did not hesitate to make extensive use of slaves during the Civil War. In some instances, railroads themselves owned slaves. Many work songs were sung to the rhythm of the swinging hammer as spikes were driven into the rails."

Huddie "Leadbelly" Ledbetter recalled hearing boogie music in Texas in 1899 and was among the first guitarists to include boogie-type bass lines in his music, while famed New Orleans trumpeter Willie "Bunk" Johnson (1879-1949) named western Louisiana as the location of his first encounter with it. Their reminiscences tend to lend credence to the testimony of veteran jazz piano players who claimed to be able to tell where a man was from by the way he played his "basses," as the various regions in the South and Midwest produced distinct stylistic variations.

The self-proclaimed "inventor" of jazz, pianist Jelly Roll Morton, said he heard boogie woogie in the 1890s when he was a lad. It was called "honky tonk" or "Texas style." The earliest reference to a term similar to boogie woogie was noted by blues and boogie pianist Sammy Price. He remembered hearing country blues guitar legend Blind Lemon Jefferson playing a moving bass line and singing about a "booger rooger," or "house rent party," around 1911. He also called the walking bass line played at 2:34 in his famous "Matchbox Blues" (1927) as a "booga rooga." It seems more than a coincidence that "boog" and "booga" are ancient African musical terms meaning "to beat." In addition, the West African word "bogi" means "to dance" while the Bantu words "mbuki-mvuki" translates as "to take off in flight… to dance wildly as if to shake off one's clothes," as apt a description as exists of the physical effect rollicking boogie woogie has on listeners!

Sheet music with "boogie" in the title appeared several times before 1900 and into the early 20th century, including "Hoogie Boogie," which John Lee Hooker later appropriated, though none contained the identifiable musical characteristics. That would not occur until 1915 with "Weary Blues" by Artie Mathews, recorded in 1919 by the Louisiana Five, a Dixieland group, as the first to feature a recognizable boogie bass line.

However, the naming of "boogie woogie," or "house rent music," is generally attributed to pioneer blues pianist Charles "Cow Cow" Davenport, who used it to describe the blues-based piano stylings of Clarence "Pine Top" Smith. In 1929, Smith waxed "Pinetop's Boogie Woogie" as the first notably commercial recording and the classic, irresistible American genre was officially christened. Joining Smith in "walking the basses" in the 1920s were his peers Davenport, Jimmy Yancey, and the young prodigy Hersal Thomas, whose "The Fives" from 1924, co-written when he was 15 years old with his brother George, was hailed as a significant influence on those who followed by none other than Meade Lux Lewis and Albert Ammons. It is a landmark in the development of the music that cannot be overestimated. The brothers are also credited with bringing boogie woogie from Texas to Chicago. Of additional significance is "Chicago Stomps" by Jimmy Blythe, also from 1924, considered the first boogie woogie to contain steady "walking" and "rolling" bass lines throughout – as opposed to "The Fives," which mixes walking lines with stride piano left-hand patterns.

1938 was arguably the watershed year in the development of boogie woogie. The "Big Three" of boogie woogie piano, Pete Johnson, Meade Lux Lewis, and Albert Ammons, who were literally and figuratively titans, commenced noticeably successful commercial recordings of the music. Lewis had previously made a name for himself with "Honky Tonk Train Blues," recorded in 1927 but released in 1930. He later appeared uncredited, playing the "devil's music," in Frank Capra's classic movie *It's a Wonderful Life* (1946). Though most piano players in any style are usually the only one on their instrument, Johnson, Lewis, and Ammons also performed and recorded in duos, as well as in a trio as the Boogie Woogie Boys, creating a spectacular, thundering sound.

Two landmark concerts called *From Spirituals to Swing*, organized by legendary producer John Hammond at Carnegie Hall in New York City in 1938 and 1939, respectively, helped ignite the boogie woogie craze that followed in the 1940s. At the first concert, all three Boogie Woogie Boys played and at the second Ammons teamed up with Big Bill Broonzy. The exposure to the public of Johnson, Lewis, and Ammons led to them taking up a popular and successful residency with blues shouter Big Joe Turner at Café Society in Greenwich Village. The club was revolutionary in many ways, not the least of which was its emphasis on presenting African-American performers, but also in having an integrated audience policy.

Boogie woogie stomped through World War II with everyone from Count Basie to Benny Goodman and the Dorsey brothers and well beyond incorporating the walking, rocking, shuffling rhythms to jitterbugging success. Mary Lou Williams and Hazel Scott were two notable women boogie woogie masters. The popular singing trio the Andrews Sisters achieved great fame with "Boogie Woogie Bugle Boy" in 1941, which later turned into a hit for Bette Midler in 1972. In 1946, pianist Jack Fina scored a pop hit by turning Rimsky-Korsakov's "Flight of the Bumble Bee" into "Bumble Boogie" in a move that would be repeated in the early 1960s. Unfortunately, by the end of the 1940s for all practical purposes, boogie woogie had run its course due to overexposure and trivialization through novelty tunes like "Chopsticks Boogie" and other crass arrangements.

However, the overarching influence of boogie woogie piano music lived on in the rock 'n' roll of the 1950s with Fats Domino, Little Richard, and Jerry Lee Lewis, to name three of the most prominent. In 1961, a group of Los Angeles session musicians formed a "fake" group called B. Bumble & the Stingers and released their own hit version of "Bumble Boogie." They followed in 1962 with "Nut Rocker," a boogie woogie arrangement of the "March" from Tchaikovsky's *Nutcracker* ballet, likewise recorded by Emerson, Lake & Palmer in 1972. Boogie versions of the *William Tell Overture* and a track titled "Dawn Cracker," based on "Morning Mood" from *Peer Gynt*, were far less successful and the "classical boogie" era ended.

Today, classic boogie woogie piano is perpetuated with an exclusive group of practitioners worldwide, notably including Arthur Migliazza. In 2012, contemporary boogie pianists Axel Zwingerberger and Ben Waters, along with drummer Charlie Watts from the Rolling Stones and bassist Dave Green, performed to great acclaim as "The A, B, C and D of Boogie Woogie."

–Dave Rubin

HOW TO USE THIS BOOK

The primary goal of this book is to teach you how to teach yourself. You want to be able to learn how to play new licks or new songs just by listening to a recording of someone else playing. To do this, you need a solid foundation in the kinds of sounds you are going to encounter in boogie woogie and blues music. By practicing and playing these sounds hundreds of times, it will not be difficult to recognize them when you hear someone else play them.

Keep this in mind: This book doesn't cover *everything*. It will introduce specific turnarounds, licks, bass patterns, etc. that you can learn and memorize and use, but more importantly it aims to teach you the *concepts* behind these things so that you can:

- Recognize new patterns when you encounter them and understand how you could use them out of their original context

- Make up your own

So, although this book isn't an encyclopedia of everything that has ever been played under the banner "Boogie Woogie Piano," it can lead you there.

This book can be as advanced or simple as you want to make it. After all, it's a book and it's not going anywhere. You can study the first few chapters, play around with them, put the book on a shelf, and pick it up again years later if you wish. Or, if you are hungry to learn, you might make it through the entire book in a month – or a week. You can always refer back to it, so don't worry about mastering everything all at once.

That being said, I had a vision in mind as I put all this down on paper. It is my *method* and it follows the way I teach my own students. I recommend that you start at the beginning and *read* each page and *try* each exercise, since I am not there next to you prompting you on what to do next. The book is laid out in a way that each chapter builds upon what came before. As you go through the book, it may not seem like this is always happening, but much like the music itself, the real important stuff is taking place subtly. For some of my students, progress is obvious, but some feel like they are not moving forward at all – until one day they look at what they are playing and say, "Six months ago I didn't even dream of doing this!" Each person walks at their own pace. Be happy with the *journey* and it won't take much time at all to reach your goals.

There is one *exception* to my urging you to work through this book from start to finish, Chapter 13 (Turnarounds, Breaks, Intros & Endings). These elements may be studied simultaneously with the licks. However, for the sake of reference, you need to have all this information in one chapter. Therefore, look at Chapter 13 after you have studied Lick #1; begin familiarizing yourself with the information there. Continue to refer to Chapter 13 throughout the rest of your studies in the book.

Each of the chapters containing the right-hand licks in Section 2 is divided into three parts. The first part is the presentation and explanation of the lick itself. The second part is called "Variations on a Theme" and contains some of the many variations you will commonly hear for the lick, but not *all* the possible variations. These are presented for the right hand only, in the key of C. It will be up to you to put them together with a left-hand bass pattern of your choosing (presented in Chapter 2) and to transpose the variations into different keys. The third part of each chapter in Section 2 is called "In the Style of…" and contains examples of how boogie woogie players use each lick in their own style. In terms of difficulty level, the first part of each chapter is *beginner*, the second is *intermediate*, and the third is *advanced*. Therefore, if you are a beginner, you can first go through the chapters in Section 2 and look only at the first part of each one, where the lick is introduced. As you get more comfortable, you can come back and look at the more advanced sections.

Whenever applicable, *listen* to the accompanying audio tracks as you are reading the musical examples. Focus your efforts on copying the way the audio is played, rather than memorizing the notes. Try to memorize the *sounds* and the emotional impression they make on you. As soon as possible, take your eyes off the page and look at your hands. Or close them and don't look at anything when you play.

If something in the book seems easy to you, or information you already know, move on to the next part. But if you are skipping around from the start, chances are you missed something that could help your playing.

Don't forget the most important element when learning something new: Hard work. Hard work is hard, but it pays off. You will get out of this book what you put in.

–Arthur Migliazza

Note: The information in gray boxes was written by Dave Rubin.

CHAPTER 1
THE TOOLS YOU WILL NEED

INTRO TO THE 12-BAR BLUES

The 12-bar blues is one of the most common chord progressions in American music and beyond. Musicians all over the world know how to play a 12-bar blues and it is usually the first chord progression they will "jam" on when meeting each other for the first time. It is simple in harmonic structure and provides a useful setting for improvisation and self-expression.

Most musicians think of the chord changes in terms of their harmonic symbols, written with Roman numerals such as I, IV, and V instead of the names of the chords. For example, in the key of C, C is the tonic (I) chord, F is the subdominant (IV) chord, and G7 is the dominant 7th (V7) chord. Therefore, when we say I, IV, and V we mean the C, F, and G chords if we are playing in the key of C. The numerals are relative to all 12 keys.

The numbers for the notes come from counting up the degrees of the major scale of the relevant key and are written as Arabic numerals. For example, play from middle C up to the next C, using only the white keys on the piano. This is a C major scale. The first note (C) is called the "root" rather than the "one;" the next note (D) is called the "2nd," and so on. If you count up to the "4th," you will be on F. The "5th" is G.

Think about notes and chords in terms of their *numbers* instead of their *letters*; it will then be easier to transpose the harmonic framework into *any key*, provided you are familiar with the major scale of that key.

There are a few standard variations on the 12-bar blues form, but this is its most basic.

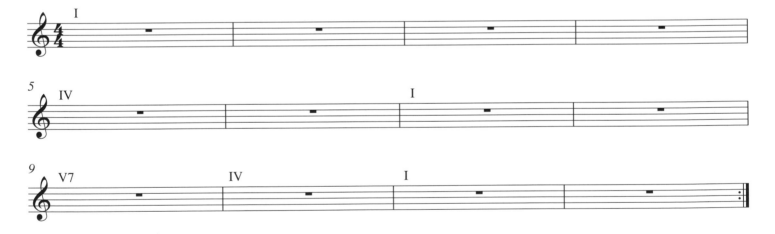

The 12-bar blues progression above is usually called the "slow change," referring to four measures of the I chord preceding the IV chord in measure 5. It is the most popular in boogie woogie music. However, for 12-bar blues there is an alternate progression known as the "fast change," in which the IV chord appears in measure 2, though it is not as common in boogie woogie piano music.

The 12-measure progression repeats throughout the piece and one repetition of 12 measures is called a *chorus*. In boogie woogie, it is more common to stay on the V7 chord for measures 9 and 10.

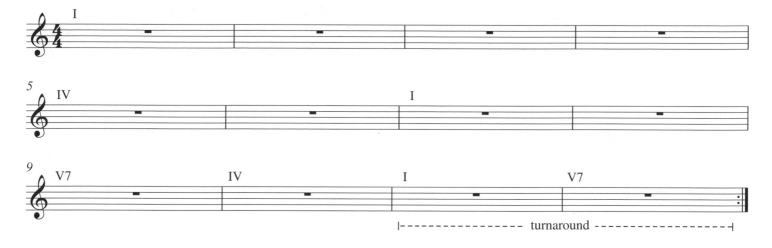

Measures 9 and 10 in a 12-bar blues, as opposed to boogie woogie music, usually contain the V and IV chords, respectively.

The last four measures are sometimes wrongly called the "turnaround," but most of the musicians I have worked with throughout my life use the word turnaround correctly to refer to getting from the I chord to the V7 chord in the last two measures of the progression. We'll look at more turnarounds in Chapter 13.

Swing Eighth Notes vs. Straight Eighth Notes

In classical music, eighth notes are accorded equal value. However, in blues and jazz music that swings, the eighth notes are slightly off-center, with the first one slightly longer in duration than the second. There are two common ways to interpret this feel in written music, as shown below. Listen to people playing swing eighth notes and imitate the sound; that's the best way to get the hang of it.

Track 1

Performance Tip: The rhythm of the two swing-eighth notes is sometimes described as "long-short." You may find it useful to think of the swing-eighth notes as being derived from triplets. The triplet rhythm is prevalent in blues and boogie woogie music and fits together well with swinging eighth notes.

Eight to the Bar: The Difference Between Boogie Woogie & Blues

People sometimes ask, "What is the difference between boogie woogie and blues?" Well, in essence, nothing. Both tend to follow a 12-bar blues progression or other common blues progressions. Both have the same harmonic elements and scales, and both were to some extent created as dance music. Boogie woogie, however, is usually played at a much faster tempo than most blues songs. Most importantly, it is a style of piano music. You can play boogie woogie on a guitar, too, but often the piano was the only entertainment an establishment had. It was the piano player's job to keep people dancing all night long. To do this, he had to have a strong left hand, and the driving rhythms he beat out came to be known as "eight to the bar." This means his left hand played eight eighth notes in every bar throughout the song. The effect is a constant driving rhythm, on top of which all kinds of other rhythms, melodies, and riffs are played. If it's in the groove, this rhythm is relentlessly compelling and causes people to start moving their bodies without even thinking about it. It works every time if it's played correctly. More on this later.

> "Eight to the bar" usually means four notes from the major scale or Mixolydian mode played in pairs, for a total of eight in each measure.

COMMON CHORDS AND HOW TO USE THEM

In blues and boogie woogie music, the major 3rd and minor 3rd are often interchangeable when singing or playing a melody, or when improvising. Sometimes the chords supporting such melodies are left "open," without a 3rd in them; but oftentimes the chords have a major 3rd implied, if not explicitly played.

> In blues vocals, guitar, and even harmonica, there is a note (microtone) between the ♭3rd and major 3rd, and between the ♭7th and major 7th, known as the true "blue note."

There are four types of chords that blues and boogie woogie piano players use most frequently:

- Major triads
- Dominant 7th chords
- 9th chords
- Major 6th chords

Major Triads

The major triad is built by going up diatonically within the major scale in thirds *twice* from the root. This will give you the root (C), 3rd (E), and 5th (G) of the chord.

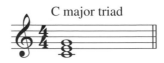

C major triad

Dominant 7th Chords

If you add one more third to the triad stack, you will get a C major 7th chord. The major 7th is rarely played in blues or boogie woogie music. Instead, we flat the natural 7th degree from the major scale one-half step, making this chord into a *dominant 7th* chord, usually written as C7.

9th Chords

If we add one more third above the ♭7th, we arrive at the 9th. Often the bottom C note is not played with this chord, because the required hand span is too large to be played by most people. The root is usually being played in the left-hand bass pattern anyway, creating a C9 chord.

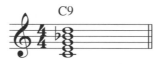

Major 6th Chords

Now let's look at our triad again. If we add the 6th (A) of the C major scale to this chord, we get a C6 chord. If we invert this chord so that the C note is on top, we get one of the most-used chord voicings in all of blues and boogie woogie music.

The triad, dominant 7th, 9th, and major 6th chords, in any number of variations or voicings, can be used interchangeably anywhere in the 12-bar blues progression at any time. It is largely your choice as to when you want to use them. Therefore, it is of paramount importance to familiarize yourself with these chords in all the keys in which you play. Learn all the inversions as well. You might practice going up and down the keyboard like so, each time putting the bottom note on top. Find a fingering that works for you.

🔊 **Track 2**

Do this sort of practice for each of the chords introduced above in – all the keys in which you normally play, even if that means just in the key of C with the C, F, and G chords for now. Make this a part of your daily practice routine until you learn the chords and their different shapes.

9th chords are frequently used for the last chord of a song. We will look at some common endings later, but here is an example.

Track 3

ADDITIONAL BLUES & BOOGIE CHORDS

Diminished 7th Chords

As seen in the previous example, a diminished 7th chord built on the tonic note may be used as a transition chord in a turnaround. It has a ♭3rd, ♭5th, and ♭♭7th. In other words, it is a chord built entirely of minor 3rds. For example, as shown, a C diminished 7th chord contains C, E♭, G♭, B♭♭ (A). A minor third up from A is C again, so the chord repeats itself. There are only three different diminished 7th chord shapes to learn because any of the four notes of the chord can be used as its root.

The diminished chord may be used to move between a major chord and a neighboring minor chord. More often it is used in a 12-bar blues in measure 6 as a ♯IV°7, following the IV chord in measure 5. It is easy to form if you are already playing the IV7 chord. For example, in a 12-bar blues in C the IV7 chord is F7, F-A-C-E♭. To make an ♯IV°7 (F♯°7) chord, simply raise the F to an F♯. Now you are playing F♯-A-C-E♭. Presto! That's a shortcut to the ♯IV diminished chord.

Minor 7th Chords

When referring to scale degrees with Roman numerals, minor chords are written with lower case symbols. For example, the I chord is written "i" if minor and the IV chord would be "iv" if minor, etc.

Minor chords and minor 7th chords are sometimes used in blues and boogie woogie music. If the tonic (i) chord is a minor 7th chord, we say we are playing a minor blues. The IV (iv) chord and even the V (v) chords may be minor 7ths as well, though customarily the V chord will be a dominant 7th. Any minor 7th chord (m7) is easily formed by flatting the 3rd of a dominant 7th chord.

II–V–I AND I–VI–II–V PROGRESSIONS

II–V–I and I–VI–II–V progressions are not necessarily an integral part of boogie woogie, but many other forms of the blues use them. You should at least be familiar with them. Once again, the Roman numerals denote degrees of the major scale, based on the I (tonic). For example, in C, a II–V–I means D (II), G (V), and C (I). These chords are frequently played as dominant 7th chords, but they can also be played as minor chords – except the V, which is always a dominant 7th chord.

There are customary places to use these progressions, but you can create an element of surprise by using them in unexpected places. The most routine is somewhere during the last four measures of the 12-bar blues. Depending on the left-hand pattern you are using (see Chapter 2), you may (or may not) be able to play through these changes without switching to another pattern temporarily. The shuffle pattern, for example, is a bad fit for playing II–V–I changes because it's too clunky to move around quickly; it also contains the 6th of the chord, which adds an unneeded harmony to the changes. However, the Yancey bass, the walking bass, and the stride bass pattern are all good choices. Here are two examples that show where you will find these chords in a 12-bar blues.

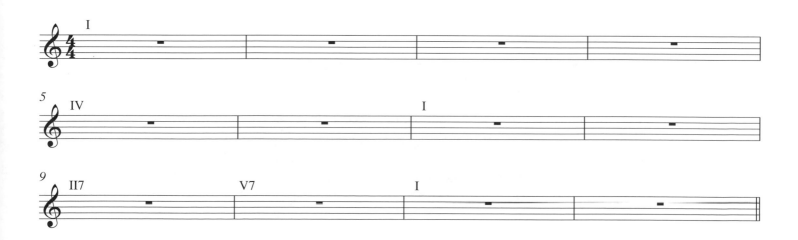

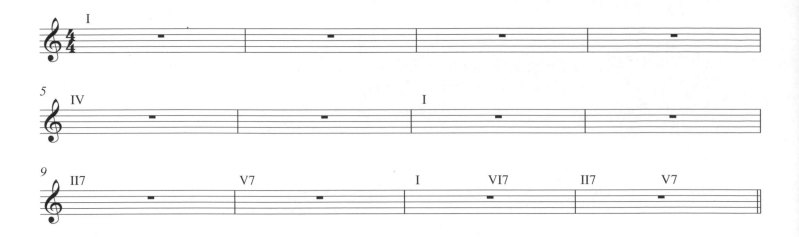

"Moon Blues" by Otis Spann, along with some versions of "Stormy Monday," are examples of II–V–I changes in a 12-bar blues progression.

The ♯V7 to V7 Variation

The ♯V (sharp five) to the V7 is another chord change repeatedly seen in blues songs. This progression occurs in measures 9 and 10, respectively, or both in measure 10. "The Thrill Is Gone" by B.B. King and "As the Years Go Passing By" by Albert King are songs that use this chord change. Coincidentally, both are "minor blues" songs.

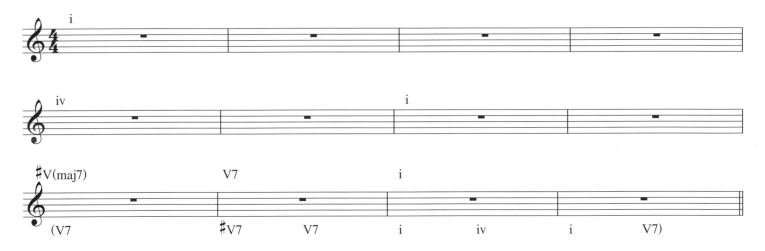

INTRODUCTION TO BLUES SCALES

Two different blues scales are used when playing or singing melodies in blues and boogie woogie music, though melodic possibilities are not limited solely to the blues scales. Boogie woogie uses mostly the "major blues scale." Only occasionally you do hear a boogie woogie song that heavily employs the "minor blues scale" – known officially as the blues scale. Blues music has tended to draw on either scale, depending mostly on time period, geographic location, and instrumentation.

The "major blues scale" is a variation of the composite blues scale, which is derived from a combination of select notes from the Mixolydian mode and the blues scale. The "minor blues scale" – or "blues scale" – is the minor pentatonic with the addition of the ♭5th, making it a hexatonic scale.

There are few real rules in blues. You can use either scale you like, usually based on whether the key of the song is major or minor. It is largely up to your discretion and taste. There are many other possibilities to draw from as a keyboard player, rather than single-note melody lines derived from blues scales. You will learn six other avenues of expression known as "licks" before finally arriving at how to use the blues scales. Teaching the blues scales first is a slippery slope because many beginning students tend to memorize them and use them exclusively when improvising on a blues form. That gets old really fast. Nevertheless, they are presented here only as a chance for you to familiarize yourself with their different sounds, so that when you listen to any blues song, you can begin to recognize which, if either, is being used.

This is the major blues scale in C.

Track 4

Here is the minor blues scale in C.

Track 5

Note that both scales include the ♭3rd, even though the suggested chord is C7. As mentioned earlier, the major 3rd and ♭3rd in blues music can often be interchanged as long as the underlying chord has a major 3rd or no 3rd. If the underlying chord is a minor chord or minor 7th chord with a ♭3rd in it, you will use only the (minor) blues scale.

There is more information about these scales and their uses in Chapter 10 (Lick #7) and Chapter 11 (Lick #8), respectively.

In classical theory, playing the ♭3rd over a major or dominant chord is generally considered "wrong," or dissonant at the least. However, in the blues, it creates a strong, "gritty" effect that is a characteristic of the music favored by blues, as well as jazz and rock, musicians.

MORE BLUES FORMS

8-Bar Blues

Not all blues songs are 12-measure progressions. The next most frequent progression is an 8-bar blues. The changes will usually be something like what follows, although there are many variations. "Tipitina," "Worried Life Blues," "Frankie and Johnnie," "Stack-O-Lee" and "The Rocking Pneumonia and the Boogie Woogie Flu" are all famous examples of 8-bar piano blues.

Tipitina; Worried Life Blues; Frankie and Johnnie

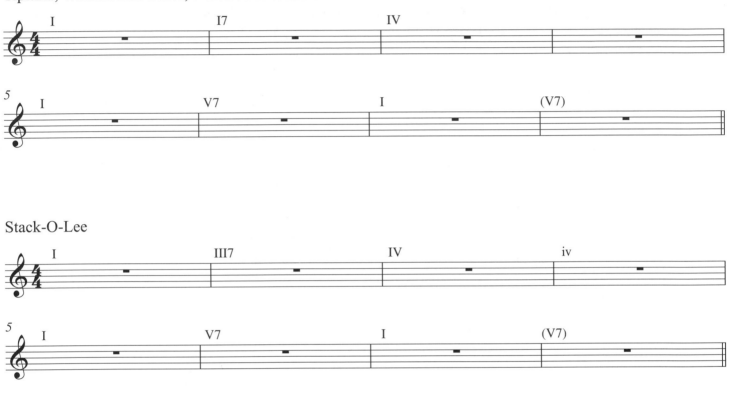

Stack-O-Lee

The Rocking Pneumonia and the Boogie Woogie Flu

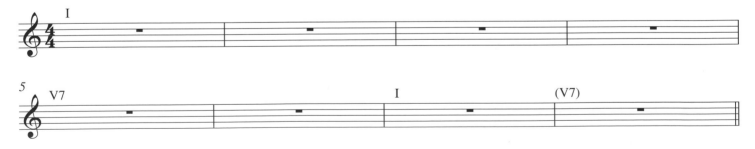

Curiously, 8-bar blues often tend to have quicker chords changes, usually after one or two measures – and virtually never four, as in 12-bar blues with the "slow change."

16-Bar Blues

The 16-bar blues is another traditional alternative to the 12-bar blues. We simply double the amount of time spent on the I chord at the beginning. "Hoochie Coochie Man" is an example of a 16-bar blues.

Hoochie Coochie Man

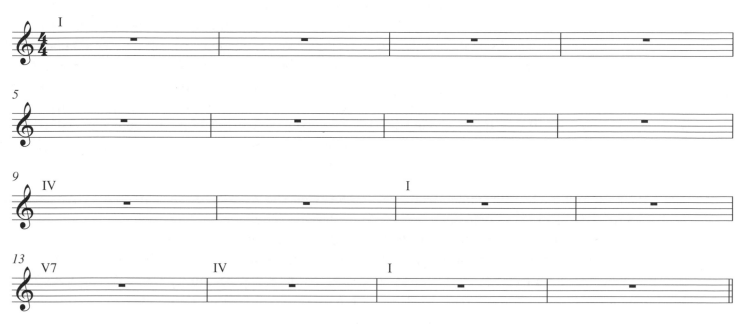

One-Chord Blues

Blues songs that stay on only one chord throughout the entire song are also often met with, though not necessarily in the boogie woogie realm. These songs may be solo-guitar-driven or played with a band. Muddy Waters and Howlin' Wolf had several songs containing one chord, such as "Mannish Boy" and "Smokestack Lightning," respectively. John Lee Hooker composed countless one-chord boogie songs accompanied only by his stomping foot.

CHAPTER 2
BASIC VOCABULARY OF LEFT-HAND BASS PATTERNS

As the title of Peter Silvester's classic work *A Left Hand Like God: A History of Boogie Woogie Piano* suggests, a boogie woogie player's left hand is their most important asset. The left hand takes the place of the bass player and drummer in a rhythm section and provides the rhythmic pulse that drives boogie woogie music. The left hand sets the tempo, the style, the groove, and the harmonic foundation upon which all the right-hand melodies and accompaniment are built. Traditionally, piano players were known for their left-hand prowess and unique bass figures. Many boogie woogie piano players took great pride in the three or four left-hand bass lines they used almost exclusively. Playing one's own unique bass pattern, or one's own take on another's bass pattern, was like putting a personal seal on the song. Almost any particular bass pattern could be played at slow, medium, or fast tempos, further increasing its scope and application.

"The most important thing in boogie woogie is the left hand." Those words were uttered by Albert Ammons, one of the kings of the boogie woogie style. It doesn't matter how fancy your right hand is, how many notes you play, or whatever. If the left hand isn't happening, there's no boogie woogie. A left-hand bass line, when played correctly, can make people move unconsciously, whether they are in a seat or on the dance floor. Just the left hand by itself! There is a lot that goes into playing it "correctly," but it can be done, and it can be powerful. There is a long tradition of people doing it where one piano player was it. And he had to make his audience, often comprised of the lowest, roughest members of society, want to dance and enjoy themselves. If he couldn't keep a steady beat, you can bet he didn't last very long. Many classic bass lines have been created over the years. Following are some of the more popular ones and the ones I use most often.

If you are new to boogie woogie, playing a repetitive left-hand bass pattern can be quite demanding physically. Muscle soreness, a burning sensation, cramping, and tension are all common symptoms when first training the left hand. They will usually disappear in a few weeks as you learn to be more efficient with your left-hand movements.

The key to efficiency and fluency is repetition. Most likely, you will be able to play these left-hand patterns after a few minutes of working on them. You'll achieve some degree of muscle memory in a couple of weeks, but mastery takes years and years of work – a lifetime, even. In other words, be patient. Enjoy the process at your own level and always strive for improvement.

PRACTICING BASS PATTERNS

Let's say you like the first left-hand bass pattern presented at the bottom of page 23. You want to learn how to play it well enough to use it in a song. Here is how to do it:

1. Memorize the pattern.

2. Play it as many times as you can every day in all the keys you will want to use it in. For example, if you want to use it in a 12-bar blues in C, then you will want to practice the bass pattern over the chords of C (I), F (IV), and G (V). When your hand *starts* to get tired, stop playing it and do something else until your hand recovers.

3. Go through the hand-independence exercises presented in the next chapter using the new bass line.

4. Play the right-hand licks you learn in this book with the new bass pattern in the left hand.

This process takes time. It won't happen overnight, but your rate of progress depends on how much time and effort you put into practicing. Be aware of your body, though, and don't push yourself too hard. Boogie woogie is an athletic event in many ways; the muscles of your hands and arms need to be conditioned and trained. At the same time, try to remain relaxed in your hands, arms, and shoulders while you play. Boogie woogie is supposed to be fun and open to interpretation, not rigid and tense. On the Internet, watch old videos of the masters: Albert Ammons, Pete Johnson, Meade Lux Lewis, Otis Spann, and Jay McShann. Do they look relaxed to you? How about when Bob Seeley plays? How about some of the contemporary players like Axel Zwingenberger, Jean-Paul Amouroux, James Booker, Dr. John, Katie Webster, Matthew Ball, Chase Garrett, Daryl Davis, and Ethan Leinwand? Do they look relaxed when they play, or rigid? How do their styles compare to the masters of old?

There is no official right or wrong way to play, but there certainly are easier and harder ways to play. Decide for yourself: Who makes it look easy? Who makes it look like a struggle? Try to hold an image of yourself playing that looks like those people you admire.

Static Patterns

What follow are several regularly played static left-hand bass patterns, divided into categories based on the styles used to refer to them. We are calling them static because, in contrast to a walking bass line, the left hand stays in the same place for the entirety of each chord change. For example, if there are four measures of C (I), the left hand stays in the same position on the keyboard to repeat its bass pattern four times before moving on. Then the hand is repositioned for the next chord and stays in that position for the entire length of that chord change.

First we have the **shuffle patterns**, where the left hand plays all eight of the eighth notes in a single measure. A blues shuffle pattern usually differs from a boogie woogie pattern in tempo only. When sped up, many shuffle patterns become boogie woogie; on the other hand, when a boogie bass form is slowed down, it becomes a shuffle pattern. Most blues shuffles are played between ♩ = 80 bpm and 120 bpm. A tempo closer to 80 bpm will be called a "slow blues shuffle," around 100 bpm will be called a "medium blues shuffle," and closer to 120 bpm will be called a "fast blues shuffle." Faster than 120 starts to sound more like a boogie woogie.

Try out these shuffle bass patterns at different tempos and see how they sound to you. Each bass pattern is one measure long. Spend time with each before moving on to the next. Find one or two favorites. The first bass pattern is used for most examples in this book. It is also the first bass pattern many boogie woogie pianists learn.

Note: Each bass pattern in the following example is played twice on the audio track, for ease in learning.

🔊 **Track 6**

Each bass pattern is presented in the key of C (I). Without too much difficulty, you should be able to transpose each into the keys or chord changes of F (IV) and G (V). Then you will be able to play a 12-bar blues.

◀)) Track 7

Next we have some of the **classic boogie woogie bass patterns** as played by Albert Ammons, Meade Lux Lewis, and Pete Johnson. This is by no means a comprehensive list. As mentioned earlier, many of the shuffle bass patterns can be sped up to become boogie woogie patterns. Most boogie woogie songs are played somewhere between ♩ = 165 bpm and 210 bpm. Try out some of these and see how they sound. Start *slowly* and gradually build up to a 165 bpm or faster. Find one or two favorites.

Note: Each bass pattern in the following example is played four times on the audio track, for ease in learning.

◀)) Track 8

Jimmy Yancey was a great innovator on the piano. His distinctive style influenced almost all the piano players who heard him. His left-hand patterns customarily contained a "broken rhythm." In other words, he didn't play a continuous stream of eighth notes in the bass. Here are two recurrently played Yancey Bass Lines. The first one (Example A) is used more for medium tempo songs (♩ = 105 bpm) and the second (Example B) for faster songs (♩ = 200 bpm).

Note: Each bass pattern is played four times on the audio track, for ease in learning.

Track 9

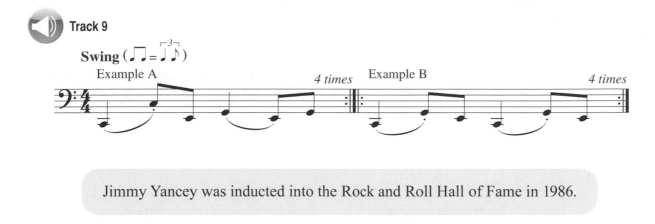

Jimmy Yancey was inducted into the Rock and Roll Hall of Fame in 1986.

Some bass patterns don't start on the downbeat of the measure, but instead have a pickup note starting on the "and" of beat 4. The effect is a slight syncopation ("surprising rhythm"), and can be fun to play. The first (Example A) is a bass pattern that is used mostly in a rock 'n' roll setting, and the second (Example B) is the same thing but with the thumb playing the tenth of the chord consistently throughout. This might be challenging if you have smaller hands. Whereas Example A is usually played at a faster tempo ($\quarternote$ = 135 bpm to 185 bpm), Example B is usually played for medium tempo songs ($\quarternote$ = 92 bpm to 108 bpm).

Note: Each bass pattern is played four times on the audio track, for ease in learning.

Track 10

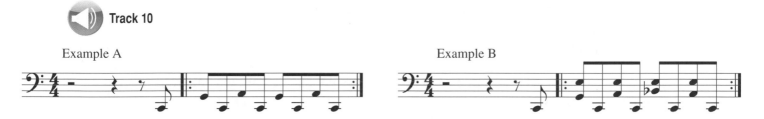

Walking Patterns

When the average person thinks of boogie woogie piano, they likely are imagining someone playing a walking bass pattern. The walking bass patterns became more commercialized in the 1940s and eventually were associated with rockabilly and jump blues. In traditional boogie woogie music, it is somewhat less prevalent than the static patterns. For one thing, it is considerably more difficult to play, and requires a different kind of muscle endurance than static patterns do. It also requires an octave stretch in the left hand. The walking bass lines can be played at any tempo, from slow blues to fast boogie. There are a number of steps you can take to build up your muscle memory for these patterns, or you can jump right in and try playing them as is. In either case, the key is to start *slowly* and gradually increase the tempo. Try them out first and then we'll discuss how to go about practicing them.

Track 11

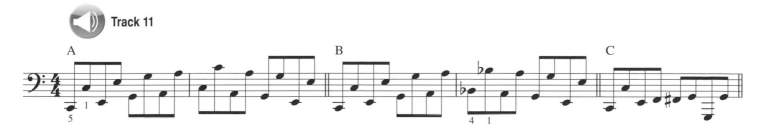

As you probably noticed, the Pattern C is somewhat static, but it is included here because of its string of single notes and octave reaches. Pattern B is only a slight variation of pattern A. Whereas A walks up to the root octave note, B walks up to the ♭7th as its highest note before descending. To develop a fluency for patterns A and B, follow these three steps.

Step 1: Using the fifth finger (pinky), play the bottom note of each octave, and rest where the top note should be played. On Pattern B, use the fourth (ring) finger to play the black note. Do this at a slow tempo; as you become more proficient, practice it with your eyes closed.

Step 2: Play the pattern in octaves, but on the quarter notes only. In other words, don't break up the octave.

Step 3: Lastly, play the pattern as it should be, starting slowly and gradually increasing the tempo. These patterns are difficult to master, so take your time and be patient.

If your hand and arm start to hurt while practicing, take a break. Because of the stretch involved, and the natural tendency for people to be tense when learning something new, this bass pattern can lead to hand and wrist tension if played too much at first. The key, as with any boogie woogie playing, is to *relax*. My hand makes almost a waving motion from the wrist when I play the walking bass patterns A and B (Track 11) It's almost as if my thumb and fingers were separated, like wearing a mitten. The top of my hand is not held up parallel to the keys as in classical music, but turned down toward my pinky finger, as if just having let go of a glass of water. Experiment with what works for you, but if you find your fingers are doing most of the work and your hand feels tense, you should try a different position.

Once you have the general idea, and can play this bass pattern without tensing your hand, it's time to start building the strength necessary to maintain this pattern for an entire song. Play the pattern at a challenging tempo. If your arm starts to burn, slow the tempo significantly and keep playing until you recover. Increase the tempo again and repeat the process. Try to keep playing by varying the tempo, but don't take your hand off the keys. When your *hand* starts to get tired, stop and take a break.

Walking Bass Pattern Transitions

The walking bass pattern allows you to walk *to* and *from* one chord to the next. There are standard ways in which people do this, but there is essentially no "wrong" way to walk between chords, as long as you get to the target chord on time.

Note: These walking transitions do not add measures to your song. They merely replace the bass pattern you normally would have played in that measure.

To the IV Chord

There are two ways in which players typically walk from the I chord to the IV chord, by either walking *up* to it or *down* to it. To walk *up* from the I chord to the IV chord in a 12-bar blues, play the transition you see in measure 4.

Track 12

(walk up to IV)

In the example above, measure 5 begins the walking pattern on the IV chord by *descending* the pattern. Changing the direction of the walking pattern can help you control your position on the keyboard and keep your hands from running into each other.

By the same token, the transition from the I chord to the IV chord can be played in measure 4 by walking *down*.

Track 13

(walk down to IV)

Half-step Walks

Half-step walks are also an easy way to make the transition from chord to chord a little smoother. Let's say you want to go to the IV chord in measure 2 of the "fast change." Play the note a half step above or below your target on beat 4 of the preceding measure.

Track 14

To the V Chord

Sometimes you will want to walk from the I chord to the V chord. Here is one way to do it.

Track 15

Staying on a Chord for Only One Measure

The full walking-bass pattern takes two measures to complete. If you have only one measure to play a chord, as in some of the examples, walking up and down the triad is one of the most conventional things to do.

New Orleans Bass Patterns

The New Orleans style of piano playing credited to Professor Longhair is an integral part of a contemporary boogie woogie piano player's repertoire. It is not the real focus of this book, but we will look at its elements from time to time. Many of the licks and notes used in this style come from earlier, more traditional styles of boogie woogie, and are easily transferrable. Here are a few New-Orleans-style left-hand patterns. Notice how the first three are not "eight to the bar," but feature a kind of syncopation, with the second note occurring on an offbeat.

Note: Each bass pattern is played four times on the audio track, for ease in learning.

Track 16

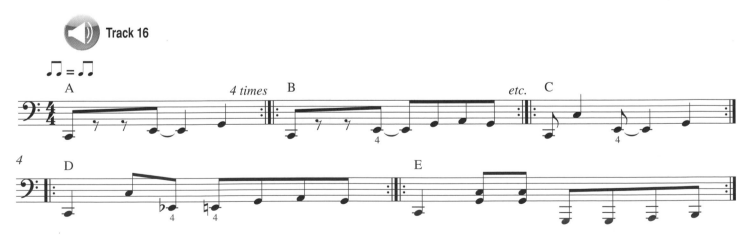

Henry "Professor Longhair" Byrd, also known as "Fess," pioneered a revolutionary style of blues-based piano combining boogie woogie and rhumba rhythms.

The Stride Pattern

The stride pattern is one of the most versatile and useful left-hand configurations you can play on the piano. Simply put, it is characterized by playing a single note on beats 1 and 3 and a chord on beats 2 and 4, creating an "oom-pah" kind of sound. It can be played slow or fast and over any kind of chord. It can also be as simple or as complicated as you want to make it. It's not necessarily a part of the boogie woogie piano style, although most boogie woogie pianists play a stride left hand to some degree. Pick a chord and alternate the root and 5th with its major triad; that's a simple way to introduce yourself to the stride style.

Track 17

James P. Johnson (1894-1955) was a pioneer of the stride piano style. His most popular and enduring composition was "Charleston" (1923).

To Swing or Not to Swing

Boogie woogie and blues can be played with either a swing-eighth-note feel or a straight-eighth-note feel. Refer to Chapter 1 for an explanation of how these differ. Play some of your favorite boogie woogie bass patterns with a straight feel and then with a swing feel. They can both groove and compel people to dance.

CHAPTER 3
ACHIEVING LEFT-HAND INDEPENDENCE

When someone hears boogie woogie music for the first time, they often think two people are playing the piano. The vast diversity of rhythms, counterrhythms, and polyrhythms seem unlikely to be coming from only one person. But this is the great magic of boogie woogie: One person sitting at a piano can sound like an entire band!

The degree to which a piano player can sound like two or more people largely depends on the degree of independence they have achieved between their hands. Our goal is to maintain a steady, in-the-groove rhythm with the left hand *no matter what we play in the right hand*. Achieving a rock-solid left hand is a function of muscle memory, which takes repetition, concentration, and dedication.

One of the charismatic things about boogie woogie and blues piano is the notion that, once you get a left-hand groove going, the rhythm becomes a blank canvas on top of which you can paint all kinds of pictures with your right hand. This is a different approach from the way most people learn pieces on the piano, which is to memorize note-for-note how the right hand fits together with the left hand. Boogie woogie piano players think of it this way: You have a left-hand bass pattern for a song and some right-hand licks you want to use; the left hand does its thing, following the chord changes of the song, while you play licks in the right hand wherever you feel them. It's that simple. The left hand is its own entity. If you are playing a shuffle-bass pattern over a 12-bar blues, that's all it does. It's like playing your own backing track. The licks you play in the right hand don't need to be in the exact same place every time you play the song.

Here is what it all boils down to: Your left-hand bass patterns need to be deeply ingrained in your muscle memory. Your left hand has to be able to do its part unconsciously. There is a series of exercises I have created to help you get a foothold in the land of hand independence. Go through these steps any time you are trying to learn a new bass line. Do them daily until they become easy, then you won't need to do them again. The method is based on introducing increasingly complex rhythms with the right hand, while trying to maintain a steady rhythm with the left hand.

Do these exercises first without a metronome, then with a metronome. *Pay attention to your left hand throughout.* Even a slight deviation from its pattern is a "mistake." Make sure the left hand does not change at all.

Track 18

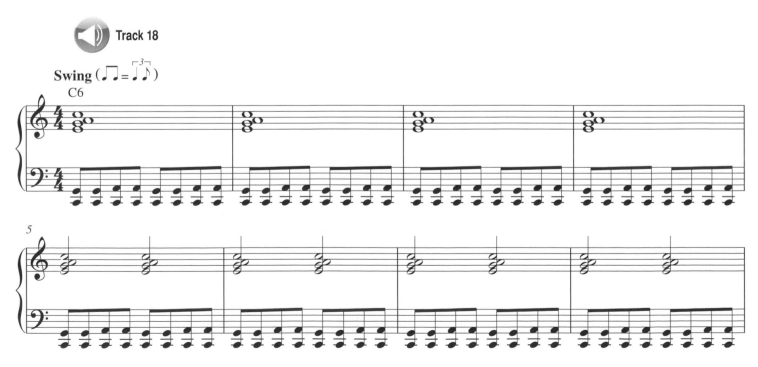

Each line of four measures should be repeated indefinitely (i.e., as long as it takes!) until you can play the right-hand rhythm with no stutters in the left hand. Only then should you move on to the next line. When the first set of exercises becomes easy, challenge yourself by playing on some of the offbeats.

Finally, challenge yourself by picking any two beats out of the four and playing on those beats with the right hand. Let's say, for example, you choose beat 1 and beat 3.

Track 19

Or, how about beat 1 and the "and" of beat 3.

Track 20

Or, the "and" of beat 1 and beat 4.

Track 21

By challenging yourself like this and creating new rhythms to play, you are breaking any chains you may create to play both hands together only in a certain way. You are freeing your left hand from your right. The next step to liberation comes by introducing various licks in the right hand to your steady left-hand bass patterns.

CHAPTER 4

LICK #1

Let's begin learning right-hand licks with what we'll call Lick #1. This is the simplest place to start. In its basic chordal structure it is a C triad (I chord) in root position that moves to an F triad (IV chord) in second inversion. Voiced in this way, the bottom note (C) is common to both chords.

Root-position chords have the root note as the lowest note in the chord. First inversions have the 3rd as the lowest note, and second inversions have the 5th as the lowest note.

To play Lick #1, simply alternate the thumb on C with the other two notes, paying close attention to the fingering. Here is **Lick #1.**

 Track 22

To give this lick a little more personality, let's add a grace note into the major 3rd (E). Use the second finger to brush off of the minor 3rd (D♯/E♭) on its way to playing the major 3rd (E). The grace notes don't alter the rhythm. Using the same finger to play more than one note in this way is sometimes called "false fingering." It is important and integral part of the blues style.

Track 23

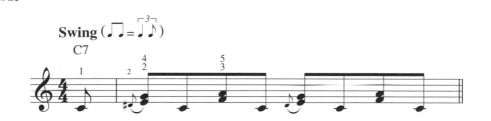

Use what you've learned to play this lick over the chords F and G. Check your results against the following examples. Track 24 is the F chord; Track 25 is the G Chord.

Track 24

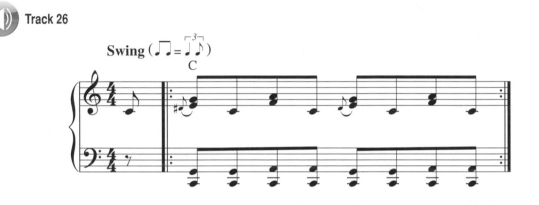

Now we want to play a lick using both hands. Choose a bass pattern for your left hand that is easy, like the shuffle pattern. Start with hands together on the C chord change. Then, when that becomes familiar, try the F and G chord changes. Transpose the left-hand bass pattern to those keys as well. Spend as much time as you need on each change before moving on. This exercise is demonstrated here on the C chord change.

Track 26

When those chords become familiar, try putting Lick #1 into the context of a 12-bar blues. Notice how the V chord (G7) is played only in measure 9 in this context. Therefore, when practicing, it is particularly important to spend time playing your licks over the V chord time and time again so that when you get there during a 12-bar blues, it will feel familiar and not take you by surprise.

Track 27

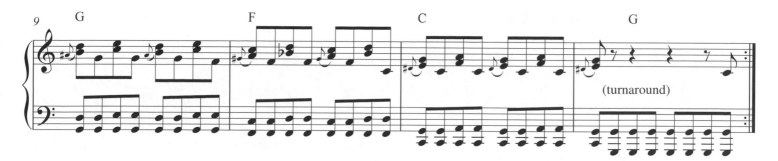

This sounds nice as is, and may legitimately be used in a real song, especially as a "comping" (accompanying) pattern. However, the real mileage from this lick comes from exploring its many variations.

Variations on a Theme

Note: The following variations are presented in the key of C. It is up to you to transpose them into the keys you wish to use them in. You can also decide what left-hand pattern you want to play.

The most oft-repeated variation you will encounter is made by continuing the pattern of ascending 3rds to the next diatonic step in the C Mixolydian mode scale. The next two steps are the 5th (G) and the ♭7th (B♭). The fingering shown here is my own, but I highly recommend learning it because it places the fourth finger on the black note (B♭) instead of the fifth finger, which is weak and unstable by comparison. Also, the fifth finger is shorter and therefore requires an awkward adjustment of the hand for it to reach. It is important to switch between the two sets of fingers on the ascending portion of the lick *only*. On the descending portion it is not so important to switch, and the third and fifth fingers can be used. This is for the purposes of speed and efficiency.

🔊 **Track 28**

Now play the root on top instead of the ♭7th. This is the other familiar extension to Lick #1. In this case, the fifth finger may be used.

🔊 **Track 29**

Here is a rhythmic variation that starts at the top of the lick and comes down.

🔊 **Track 30**

And again with the root on top.

Track 31

Other variations can be derived by mixing up the order of the notes and the rhythm.

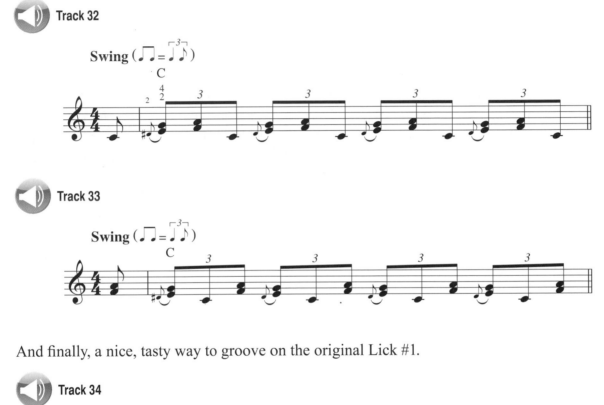

Track 32

Track 33

And finally, a nice, tasty way to groove on the original Lick #1.

Track 34

These are by no means all the possible variations on Lick #1. They are, however, some of the more pervasive ones, enough to get you started on making this lick a part of your musical vocabulary. You should also be able to recognize the lick when you hear another player use it. Now let's take a look at how some other pianists have used Lick #1 in their own styles.

In the Style of...

Lick #1 is one of the most widely known right-hand phrases you will hear in the boogie woogie and blues piano tradition. From the earliest players of the style to the most contemporary, from New Orleans to Detroit, everyone has their own approach to this lick. First, let's look at how Clarence "Pinetop" Smith sometimes played it. (We'll talk more about him in the next chapter.) Here, the 3rds are continued downward instead of upward, yielding a nice little "period" to the statement of the lick. The following example represents the first four measures of a 12-bar blues in G.

"Way Down Yonder in New Orleans," Huey "Piano" Smith was playing it, too – in a funky kind of way – with a syncopated straight-eighth-note feel. It uses all the same notes, but in different places and rhythms.

Track 36

(turnaround)

Katie Webster's playing offers some great examples of how to get a lot of mileage out of Lick #1. She personifies a more contemporary boogie woogie player. Her version adds a lot of flash to this pattern.

Track 37

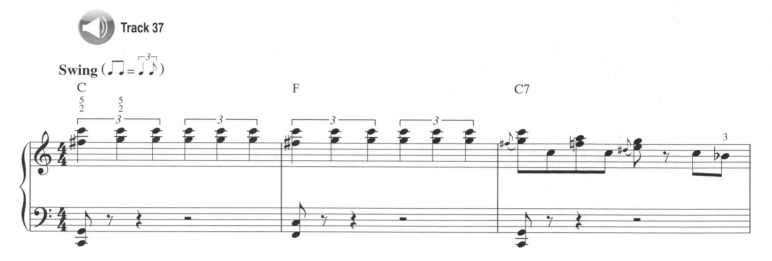

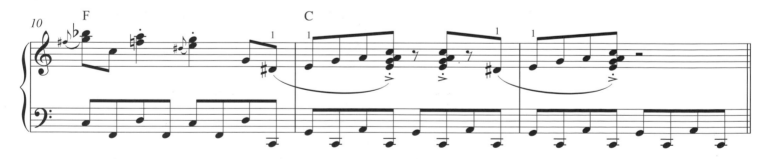

Allow yourself time to become familiar with Lick #1. Spend at least a week practicing these variations with different bass patterns. You can take the bass lines from the examples in this chapter or from the list of bass patterns contained in Chapter 2. If you want to challenge yourself, try them in different keys as well.

Do you find that certain variations fall under your fingers more easily than others? Do certain variations catch your ear? First learn the ones you are most interested in. Become familiar with them. Make them part of your vocabulary so you can use them in any song you choose.

When you get Lick #1 under your fingers, it's time to move on to Lick #2.

The "Pinetop Lick"

This is called the "Pinetop Lick" because it was first popularized in the 1928 song "Pinetop's Boogie Woogie." Most likely, it was used for decades before that. Next to Lick #1, it is probably the most widely used pattern in boogie woogie and blues piano. There are many different ways to approach it, and every piano player of the style has their favorites. Let's meet it in its most basic form and then look at some of its classic variations.

The C9 Chord

Fundamentally, Lick #2 is based around a C9 chord. Play a C (root) with your left hand, then build the rest of the chord with your right hand, starting with your first finger (thumb) on E (3rd) and going up in 3rds from there. Continue until you get to the ninth degree (D) of the C major scale, remembering to flat the 7th (B♭) of the chord. To play the chord with right hand only, place your thumb on C, second finger on E, third finger on G, fourth finger on B♭, and fifth finger on D. It's a powerful position and a powerful chord. Play it a few times to get it under your hand.

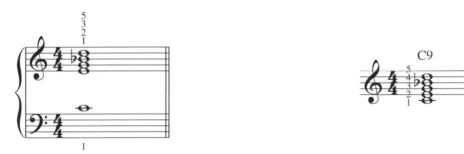

Lick #2 is played by basically breaking up this chord between the first finger (thumb) and the top notes of the chord, similar to Lick #1. It includes three pickup notes before the downbeat, which start a whole step below the 3rd (E) of the C9 chord. Keep that in mind as you play through the musical figure. It's a formula you can memorize. The pickup notes start a whole step below the C9 chord. Once you get to the first finger (thumb) on the bottom note of the chord, open your hand to the full position of the chord and you will be ready to play.

Note: The pattern is given twice in the example below.

Use the same formula to find Lick #2 over the IV (F) and V (G) chords of the C blues. You'll need to figure out how to play an F9 chord and G9 chord first; don't forget about the ♭7th degree. When you've got those chords worked out, apply the formula for playing Lick #2, then check your work with the following examples.

Note: The pattern is given twice in the examples below.

Now play Lick #2 with the left-hand shuffle bass pattern. Start with the bass line and then begin to introduce the lick. At first play it in C (I), F (IV), and G (V), practicing these changes separately for a while.

Be aware that pickup notes are played *before* the downbeat of the measure. In a case like the exercise above, where you are repeating the lick over and over, the pickup notes are replayed at the end of every measure to lead you back to the lick again. The *last* time you want to play the lick, do not play the pickup notes following the lick. Instead, leave the right hand silent on beats "and four and."

Take your time. Spend five minutes on each key and build up to ten minutes. Get into it and appreciate it so the time spent doesn't matter to you. Have fun with the process; that's the key. The more you enjoy it, the more you will own it and it will be yours for life.

Once you are comfortable playing this lick while maintaining the shuffle-bass pattern in the left hand in C, F, and G, practice it in the 12-bar blues context.

Track 42

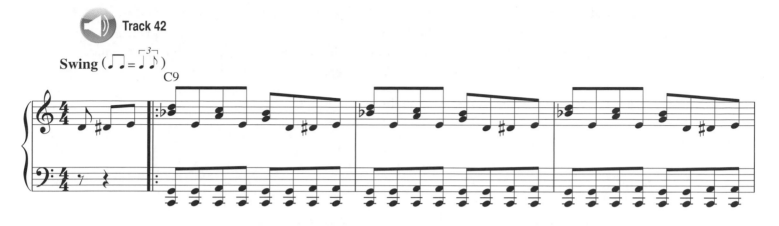

Variations on a Theme

The first variation of Lick #2 is every bit as common as the way it was originally presented. And, much like the first variation of Lick #1, it consists of a slight extension on the top notes of the lick. So, instead of starting with the ♭7th (B♭) and 9th (D) on top, go to the octave (C) and 3rd (E). After that, there's the same descent in 3rds. Also, the pickup note is clipped to make room for these extra notes on top. Slide your thumb from the D♯ to the E to make the repeating of this lick more efficient.

Note: The pattern is given twice in the example below.

Track 43

The next variation is similar to the original lick, but with a quick little half-step turn in it.

Note: The pattern is given twice in the example below.

Track 44

The last variation is usually not thought of as the same lick because it sounds so different. But if you look closely, you'll see it has exactly the same notes – with their positions inverted. Can you can see it as the same pattern? It is one of my favorite ways to play this lick. It can be used rhythmically in a boogie woogie, but it also sounds full of soul if played at a slow blues tempo.

Note: The pattern is given twice in the example below.

Track 45

Now it is up to you to practice these variations for the F and G chord changes, using the same processes you have been learning by transposing the original lick. This is important to do. Learning how to transpose the licks by using your brain, instead of reading them on a page, is what separates those who can have fun with these licks and use them at will in their own playing from those who must always play them the same way they learned them on paper. So spend some time and get to know Lick #2 and its variations. They are simple, and when they "click," they will be yours.

In the Style of...

How might Clarence "Pinetop" Smith – one of the fathers of the boogie woogie style – use these licks in his playing? A couple of possibilities are shown in the examples that follow. Just for fun, I've changed the bass lines to ones Pinetop might use.

Track 46

Can you recognize that the variations are based on Lick #2? There will be small differences in each player's rendition of the lick, but once you know the basic structure, you can see and hear it easily. The important thing is to take your time. Challenge yourself, but don't be too hard on yourself either. Do the best you can and enjoy them at whatever stage your abilities allow. Progress requires a delicate balance between patience and enjoyment of the path, and a desire to improve.

Once you have spent time with Lick #2 (Days? Weeks? Months?) and feel like you have a good grasp of it, it's time to move on to Lick #3.

The "Jimmy Yancey Lick"

If Lick #2 is sometimes referred to as the "Pinetop Lick," then we might be justified in calling Lick #3 the "Yancey Lick." Prevalent in many of Jimmy Yancey's songs, although it probably predates him by 50 years, this lick is now a staple of the boogie woogie and blues piano tradition. Its sound is timeless; you will recognize it immediately if you have listened to anyone play piano in this style. Its basic structure is a C chord descending to another C chord.

By inserting a series of half steps, we get **Lick #3**.

Can you recognize the pattern or formula? Do you see how the lick starts a half step below the first C chord and then eventually comes down through half steps and one whole step to get to the second C chord? Meanwhile, it pivots off the root of the chord in the middle.

Apply what you already know to play this lick in F and G. G is nearly identical to C in terms of its shape, but F is a little snaky, so be careful. After you have figured them out, check your work.

Notice how the same fingering can be used for all three chord changes. Now let's put Lick #3 in C (I) with our shuffle bass line. Remember to practice this in F (IV) and G (V) as well.

Track 51

Once you are familiar with Lick #3 in C, F, and G – and how it fits with the left-hand shuffle pattern – try it in a 12-bar blues context. Take note that because Lick #3 takes two measures to complete, you need to stay on the G (V) for two bars and skip the F (IV) in measures 9–10.

Track 52

For 30 years, Jimmy Yancey was a groundskeeper for the White Sox at old Comiskey Park in Chicago. One wonders how many of his co-workers knew they should be humbled to have a legendary boogie woogie piano player in their midst.

Variations on a Theme

The first of the variations I will present here is simply the result of inverting the 6ths to become 3rds. In other words, the notes are exactly the same, but what was the lower note of each chord is now the higher note. I use the "false fingering" technique to play this one. Playing this lick in 3rds is extremely important in the boogie woogie style. It will come up time and time again the more you listen to this music and try to play it.

Track 53

The next variation of Lick #3 is made simply by breaking up the 6th intervals into a triplet pattern. It is used again and again. The fingering you used for the original lick can be applied here as well.

Track 54

Lastly, if you play the notes of Lick #3 in 3rds again, you will hear a way it is often played. The fingering is my own. I find the second and fourth fingers to be the strongest for playing in this manner. Notice how, on the ascent, there is a quick switch of fingers, similar to what you learned with Lick #1, which I recommend for the sake of speed and accuracy.

Track 55

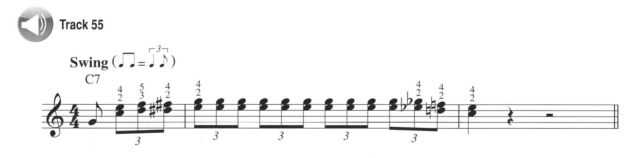

This is a relatively simple lick, but it has wide-reaching applications in both boogie woogie and blues music. Spend as much time as you need to become familiar with Lick #3 and its variations.

In the Style of...

Let's look at how other players might approach Lick #3, starting with Jimmy Yancey. In this example, notice how the entire lick is *not* transposed to the F and G chords, but simply used in a different way, while maintaining its C position.

Albert Ammons, in his version of the Hersal Thomas classic "Suitcase Blues," uses the lick in 3rds, a technique you have already learned.

Track 57

Pinetop Smith taught Albert Ammons his "Pinetop's Boogie Woogie." Ammons later recast it as "Boogie Woogie Stomp" and recorded in 1939. Ammons performed at the inaugural celebration for President Harry S. Truman in January 1949.

Many of the boogie woogie players in the late 1930s and 1940s, especially Albert Ammons, Pete Johnson, and Meade Lux Lewis, used this lick in their faster tunes as well. A stock-in-trade embellishment of theirs is to alternate rapidly back and forth between the top two half steps of the lick. When I do this, I use the third and fifth fingers for each half step, respectively. It might seem strange to do this at first, but it works for me at any tempo. Experiment with your own fingering on Pete Johnson's version.

Track 58

Spend time analyzing and practicing Lick #3 and its variations. The payoff from familiarizing yourself with this simple lick will be enormous. Take as much time you need and have fun with it. When you are ready, move on to Lick #4.

The C6 Chord

Lick #4 is almost too obvious to mention, but it is such a part of this music that it needs to be recognized as a separate lick. Basically it is a C6 chord, the same C6 chord we learned for the hand coordination exercise in Chapter 3.

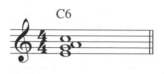

Keep your hand in that C6 shape and try rolling your fingers down all the notes. Maintain the same hand position as you're doing the roll, so it becomes a hand roll initiated by the wrist rather than a finger movement. If you roll down to the ♭3rd (E♭/D♯) instead of the natural 3rd (E) first with the first finger, then slide the first finger up to the natural 3rd, then you've got **Lick #4**.

Now transpose Lick #4 to the F (IV) and G (V) chord changes. Start by finding the F6 and G6 chords and then break them up into the lick. Check your results against the examples.

Next let's put hands together and practice this lick with the shuffle bass pattern for the C (I), F (IV), and G (V) chord changes. The following example is over C, so it will be up to you to transpose the exercise to F and G.

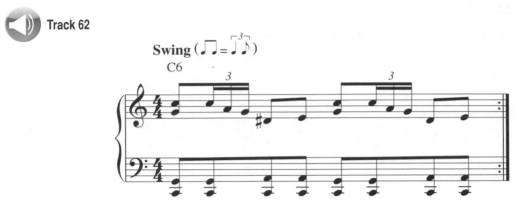

When you are familiar with Lick #4 in C, F, and G, play it in a 12-bar blues context.

Remember, if you are having trouble making the transitions between chords smoothly, practice moving between the chords over and over. Try this, using the 12-bar blues above: Start with the left hand and make sure you can transition without a break in the rhythm. Then introduce the right hand. Play two measures on C and two measures on F. Repeat until you can play both hands together smoothly. Then try C for two measures, G for two measures, and back to C, etc. In this way, you can drill your weak points until they are no longer weak points.

If coordinating Lick #4 with a left-hand pattern is still proving to be tricky, try this easier version first, in which you play only the eighth notes of Lick #4.

 Track 64

Variations on a Theme

There aren't a lot of variations for Lick #4. Nevertheless, the ones that do exist get used by everyone, regardless of instrument.

Since this lick uses a downward rolling sound, a logical question might be, "What would it sound like if I rolled it up instead?" That leads us to one of the most widely used licks in all American music – from blues and ragtime to boogie woogie, gospel, jazz, Dixieland, stride, rock 'n' roll, R&B, soul, funk, bluegrass… you name it.

When the direction of the lick is reversed, the same fingers can be used on the way up as were used on the way down in the original.

 Track 65

If you combine the upward rolling variation with the downward rolling variation, another common lick emerges.

Track 66

Use all the licks and variations you are learning. That's the best way to make them a part of your musical vocabulary. And the *only* way you can *use* them is to *know* them. This means your hands know by muscle memory how to play a lick without having to consciously think about it. The memory of how it *sounds* is the only part of playing the lick that needs to be in the consciousness. When people say, "I play what I hear in my head," they are saying they simply have to recall the sounds of *what their hands already know how to do*. Then their hands go through the motions while they are *hearing* what they want to play next.

Most improvisation is produced in this manner. Only rarely will someone on stage play something they have *never* played before, something completely spontaneous that was not a part of their muscle memory and licks vocabulary.

Therefore, make these licks part of your muscle memory by practicing them with the right hand only, then with all your favorite bass lines. Be creative and challenge yourself! What if you want to use the licks in a key besides C? First practice the licks in the keys you normally play in, then see what they feel like in the ones you don't normally use. If you can play a 12-bar blues only in C at this point, you might want to explore other common keys like F, G, B♭, E♭, E, A, and D. It's not as hard as you might think. For example, if you learn the lick in the key of C with the C (I), F (IV), and G (V) chords, then playing a blues in F with the F (I), B♭ (IV), and C (V) chords requires you learning only one more chord: B♭.

In the Style of...

The pattern of Lick #4 is ubiquitous in boogie woogie. You probably had heard it prior to reading about it here. You may not have been aware that you had heard it, but chances are that since you have been introduced to it now, you will notice it all over the place. Here is how one of my favorite piano players, Big Maceo Merriweather, sometimes used it.

CHAPTER 8

LICK #5

In terms of complexity, **Lick #5** is probably the simplest of all of the licks. It is just four notes repeated over and over, yet it is one of the most difficult to play. The reason is the fingering. In this lick I will show you how to master another level of the "false fingering" technique introduced earlier, where the same finger is used to play two adjacent notes. Here, the third finger plays the first two 16th notes of the lick. The real trick is to play these four notes in such a clear and even way as to *sound* like you are playing them with four fingers instead of three.

For practice, set your metronome to ♩ = 65 bpm and play Lick #5 using *four* fingers by placing your fourth finger on the E♭ and using your third finger on the D. Do this about ten times or so, striving to play the 16th notes as evenly as possible. When you have that sound in your ear, switch to using *three* fingers. Can you make the three-finger version sound as clear and even as the four-finger version? With the metronome clicking, switch back and forth between fingerings and listen for any difference between the two. There shouldn't be any.

When 65 bpm becomes comfortable, increase the speed gradually. To use this lick in a boogie woogie, you should be able to at least play it at 190 bpm. My max is about 250 bpm, but at that point it becomes somewhat of a blur and would be used only as an "effect" rather than a melodic idea. If you are losing track of the 16th notes as you get faster, focus on playing your third finger on E♭ at every quarter note. Practice the lick slowly enough times that the motion is programmed into your muscle memory. The rest of the lick will then play itself, provided you start at the right time with the third finger on every quarter note.

Putting Lick #5 into a swinging boogie woogie or blues context raises an interesting question: How can you swing a 16th note? Usually, eighth notes are the only subdivision of a beat that are swung. It's true, 16th notes can't be swung, but that doesn't prevent us from using Lick #5 in a swing context and here's why: As the tempo gets faster and faster, it becomes impossible to swing even an eighth note. This phenomenon occurs around 220 bpm for the quarter note where everything starts to flatten out. There is also a kind of "grey zone" in which the ear forgives the sound of one hand swinging and the other one not. It comes out sounding pretty cool. This zone is for a quarter note of about 180 bpm to about 220 bpm; most boogie woogies are played in this "grey zone."

If you are playing a slow blues, or any song that is slower than 180 bpm, then Lick #5 should be played somewhat out of time by not adhering to a predictable rhythm – or by making the first of the four notes fall on a quarter-note triplet.

Do an Internet search to find an audio clip of Avery Parrish playing his variation of this lick in the third chorus of "After Hours," recorded with the Erskine Hawkins Orchestra in 1940. If you are going to play the lick "out of time," you need to have both your left-hand bass pattern and Lick #5 in your muscle memory. That way, you can guide the lick simply by imagining the way you want it to sound.

Try Lick #5 with an accompanying left-hand pattern now. For fun, let's employ one that could be used as both a shuffle pattern and a boogie woogie pattern.

Note: The audio track has two parts, with four measures of the left hand playing straight eighth notes and four measures of the left hand playing swing eighth notes.

In the 1940s, "After Hours" became affectionately known as "The Negro National Anthem." It still stands today as a revered classic.

Harmonically speaking, Lick #5 is one of those "magic licks" you do not need to transpose for the IV and V chords. It simply works *as is* over all three chord changes. For the sake of practice, let's play it over the entire 12-bar blues form, something you may (or may not) wish to do onstage. Start by playing the following figure as straight eighth notes in both hands. Don't swing anything – just fit the 16th notes of the right hand exactly with the eighth notes of the left. After you get familiar with playing your hands together, then try to swing the left hand.

(turnaround)

Repeating a hip riff or lick identically over an entire 12-bar blues progression is a great improvisational tool for building musical tension. The technique is often used in blues, rock 'n' roll, and rockabilly. Be aware that it sounds different over the IV and V chords because the underlying harmony changes.

Variations on a Theme

The most common variations of Lick #5 either add a note to the top of the lick or reverse the order of the notes. Adding a note on top might sound like this.

Track 71

Reversing the order of the notes, going from bottom to top, might sound like this.

Track 72

Just for fun, here is the first blues progression I ever learned. I was ten years old and living in Maryland. My teacher was Judy Luis-Watson.

Track 73

(turnaround)

In the Style of...

A great use for Lick #5 comes from the Queen of Boogie Woogie piano herself, Hadda Brooks. Here are a couple of ways she played the lick.

Track 74

Track 75

CHAPTER 9

LICK #6

Lick #6 is linear, almost scale-like in form. An essential lick in the boogie woogie and blues tradition, almost every piano player has used it – or something like it. I first learned its basic shape when I was learning how to play "After Hours," because it occurs in the second chorus of the song.

The fingering I suggest here is my own; although it looks strange, I have found this to be easiest because there is no crossing under of the first finger. Start with this, but if you find you like another fingering better, use it. In most cases, there is no "correct" fingering for boogie woogie or blues piano. Of course, playing the lick for the IV and V chords, as well as in other keys, will require different fingering. Here is **Lick #6** in C. Play through it a few times to get a feel for it.

Track 76

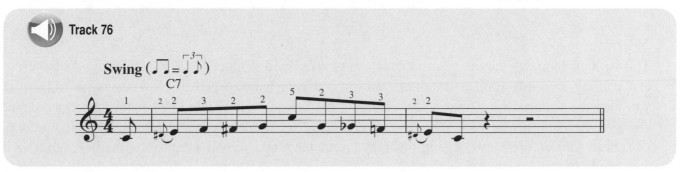

Now see if you can figure this lick out in F (IV) and G (V), then check your results. Note how the F fingering is a little different, but still arbitrary and my own suggestion.

Track 77

Track 78

After playing Lick #6 a few times in each key, put both hands together with the shuffle bass pattern as shown. Try this over and over again – about 15 times – in C, F, and G.

Track 79

This isn't the hippest-sounding phrase, but it isn't the finished product yet. You're learning the fingering and gaining a simple context in which you can put your hands together. Now see what happens if you play the pattern in a 12-bar blues, changing the lick to F (IV) and G (V) according to the chord changes. Remember that Lick #6 takes two measures to complete, so you will need to stay on the G (V) chord for two measures. Again, this may not be the way you will want to use the lick, but give it a try anyhow.

Track 80

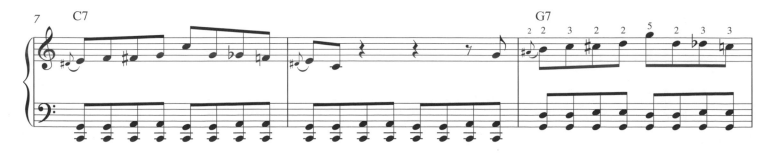

(turnaround)

Variations on a Theme

This first variation is the way you will usually hear Lick #6 phrased, with the pickup notes played as a triplet rhythm.

Track 81

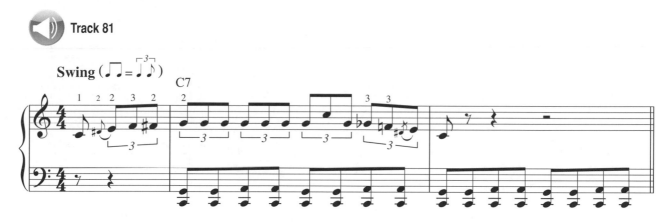

The second finger is used to play the repeated G notes because it is a strong and stable finger. This is another reason I introduced Lick #6 with the second finger playing the G, even though it wasn't being repeated in the original lick. If your second finger is accustomed to having that note covered, then it's ready to repeat it if you choose to do so in the moment.

Using the same finger to play a repeated note goes against most conventional teachings of piano technique, but the blues isn't about having flashy or mechanically perfected technique. The blues is about making the instrument sing and talk like a human voice. So, in a symbolic way, when you use the same finger to play one note repeatedly, you may have to respond to your hand getting tired or being inconsistent with the rhythm, two factors that will give your playing a unique personality of its own, a personality that will develop and change over time as you become familiar with using the piano as a means of self-expression.

Another benefit of using the second finger to play the repeated G is that it leaves the rest of your hand open to play other notes at the same time, such as keeping the octave on top with the fifth finger.

Track 82

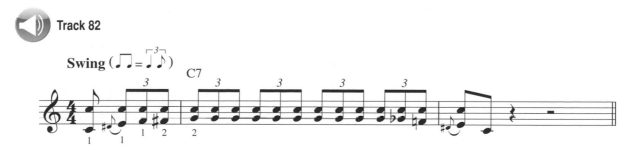

In the Style of...

One of the most famous and widely copied instances of Lick #6 is in the second chorus of "After Hours" as played by Avery Parrish. The following example is an approximation. Notice how the pickup notes are not a triplet figure as before, but instead are 16th notes. This subtle change is yet another variation on the phrasing of Lick #6. There is no one right way or wrong way to play it; I often use either or both in the same song.

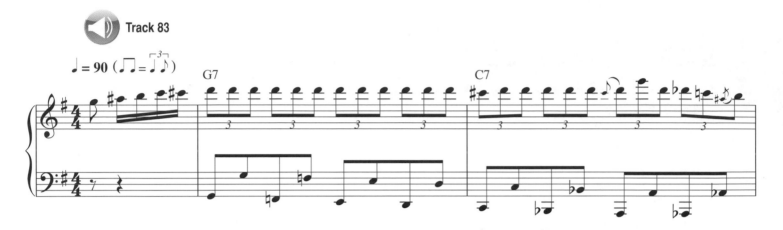

Composite Blues Scale and Major Blues Scale

The final two licks are scales. Many people tend to learn a blues scale and then rely on it for improvisation. They don't find out how to use the scale properly or pick up any other licks or elements of the blues style. That's why I have waited until now to talk about the scales in depth.

However, blues scales are completely legitimate and can be quite convincing if used in combination with the other licks you have already become familiar with.

Lick #7 is what we call the **major blues scale** because it is closely related to the major pentatonic scale. It is also referred to as a "composite blues scale" because, as explained in Chapter 1, it is a combination of select notes from the blues scale and the Mixolydian mode. I tend to think of it as the major pentatonic scale with the addition of the ♭3rd.

For reference, here is the major pentatonic scale. As the name suggests, this scale has only five notes

Fingering is an issue that arises with both the pentatonic and the blues scale. There are a few different options for these scales; the one you choose depends largely on the context in which you are playing the scale. For example, are you playing the entire scale as a descending run, or are you playing only a part of the scale as a segue to another lick? In general, for both scales use only the first three fingers of your right hand, whether going up or down the scale. The fingerings I suggest here will get you started. To go up more than one octave, simply put your thumb back on the C when you get to the top of the scale. You will be in position to play another octave.

Try figuring out the major blues scales in F and G (given below), and any other keys you frequently play in or want to play in. They will be a useful tool and can be applied to almost any style of music you are playing.

Track 86

Track 87

Variations on a Theme

Build licks based on fragments of the composite blues scale. This is the best way to incorporate it into your playing – not by using it as a scale. We've already encountered licks based on this scale in Tracks 59, 65, 68, and 72.

Visualize the root as a center point or a final resting point, rather than a *starting point*. That's a good way to get your mind to break out of thinking of these notes as a scale. For example, put your first finger on G and walk up the scale to A and C.

Now go two notes up the scale from the C and start on E♭. Play E♭ with your third finger and walk down the scale to C, playing E♭, D, and C. This is how you surround the root with your phrase, starting below and above the root, where you will eventually end up.

For example, look how we can surround the C with these phrases. Now it no longer sounds like we're just playing a scale.

Track 88

Many licks and melodic lines can be made from the notes of the major blues scale. Even today, the majority of songs written with mass appeal – be they blues, folk, country, pop, rock, R&B, or anything in between – use melodies based primarily on this scale. The more you become familiar with it, the more you will be able to recognize it in songs.

The major blues scale has a twin sister. I call it a twin because it is essentially the same scale, but with a different tonic. If you know about relative major and minor keys, this will make sense. Here is a brief description.

Every major key in Western music has a minor key that shares the same key signature. These two keys are said to be in a *relative relationship*. The tonic of the relative minor resides three semitones (half steps) below the tonic of the relative major. For example, A is three semitones below C, and A minor is called the *relative minor* of C major.

If you play the C major scale starting on the A note and ending on the next A note, then you have played the A natural minor scale or Aeolian mode. In both cases, the major and minor keys share the same key signature and *exactly* the same notes.

Track 89

Using this knowledge of relative major and minor, we can easily translate this formula to the blues scales. Since A minor is the relative minor of C major, play the C major blues scale exactly as shown previously, but this time starting on the note A. Play the scale until you reach the next A, then come back down.

Track 90

You have just played the A blues scale, or what we call the "A minor blues scale." All the notes of the scale are the same; the only difference is that there is a new tonic (A). This essentially cuts in half the workload of learning the blues scales, because each scale can be used as a major *or* minor, depending on the key.

Theoretically, the minor blues scale may be applied the same way as the minor pentatonic scale, used extensively in both major and minor key blues and rock songs. This practice in "popular music" is an intriguing topic. As mentioned earlier (page 19), classical music and jazz (which is not blues-based) virtually never employ a ♭3rd melody note, which is considered related to minor chords or keys, in a major key composition. However, our ears have become acclimated to the appealingly "nasty" sound, having heard the ♭3rd in major key progressions and blues and rock songs over many decades.

In the next chapter, we'll look at some potent ways to use this minor blues scale.

This is the last of the eight licks, the **minor blues scale**. As mentioned at the beginning of Lick #7, the blues scales tend to be overused by beginners to the style. As you have now seen, piano players have much more available to them than playing single-note lines based on a blues scale. However, the blues scale has its place and can be powerful in evoking emotional responses, especially when used *sparingly*.

Here is the C minor blues scale. The fingering may look strange, but it's the one I use. Notice that it's a little different on the descending portion of the scale.

Note: It's also possible to play this scale using only the second and third fingers.

The minor blues scale is based largely on the minor pentatonic scale. It shares all the same notes and adds an extra one: the F♯ (G♭). This sixth note is the gritty ♭5th and is sometimes called a "blue note."

Minor Pentatonic Scale

As with the major blues scale and major pentatonic scale, the fingering is largely subjective. It is usually adapted to the context, such as some kind of descending run or as a segue to another lick, etc. Don't worry too much about fancy fingering, just do what feels natural. I will give my suggested fingerings as a starting place for your own experimentation.

Important: Unlike the major blues scales and major pentatonic scales, minor scales do *not* need to be transposed to the key of each chord change in the blues unless you are playing a minor key blues. In other words, if you are playing a blues in C, then the C minor blues scale will work over the C7 chord, the F7 chord, and the G7 chord if you select the proper notes – especially the root of the IV (F) and V (G), which appear in the C minor pentatonic scale. In fact, it would sound odd if you played each chord's respective minor blues scale in a major key song or progression.

Exercises/Drills

Before we get into licks using the minor blues scale, here are two exercises you can do to familiarize yourself with the layout of the *pentatonic* scales. You won't find sounds like this in early percussive boogie woogie music; they occur later on in the music of players like Otis Spann and James Booker, who use linear scale ideas more often. You might recognize how having these exercises under your fingers can help.

The exercises that follow should be done with a metronome. Strive for evenness and clarity throughout. Start as slowly as you need to; repeat those sections where the fingering is difficult for you until muscle memory takes over. Gradually increase the metronome speed until you reach a level at which you are happy. On the audio track, each exercise is demonstrated at a slow tempo and a fast tempo.

The first exercise consists of going up and down the scale in clusters of three notes. Look at the pattern after the second C is played; you can see the three-note cluster in the ascending pattern. The descending cluster pattern is already apparent.

Note: On the audio track, the example is played first at 75 bpm, then at 175 bpm.

Track 93

The second exercise goes up and down in clusters of four notes.

Note: On the audio track, the example is played first at 75 bpm, then at 150 bpm.

Track 94

Variations on a Theme

As with the major blues scale, construct licks based on fragments of the scale. That's the best way to incorporate it into your playing. The first fragment is the equivalent of what we played with Lick #5, but in the minor blues scale context. And the same fingering of three fingers for four notes will be used.

Track 95

Articulate the notes in Track 95 as evenly as possible, so that it sounds as clear as if you were playing with four fingers. Start slowly, with the metronome at 60 bpm; gradually increase the speed until you can play it as fast as you want to. When the lick gets super fast, it becomes a blur and is heard more as an effect than a melodic line.

In the same vein, here are two more variations you'll sometimes hear. Pay attention to the fingering.

Track 96

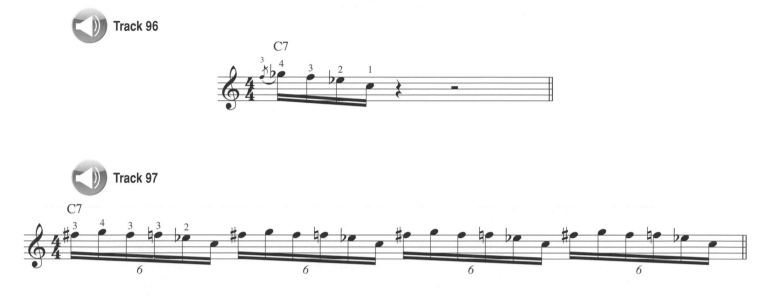

Track 97

If the thumb is on C and the other fingers reaching E♭, F, and G can be thought of as the *bottom* position to playing this scale, then the second finger on G and the fourth finger on B♭ and the fifth finger on the high C can be thought of as the *top* position. From this position there is another lick/fragment that is commonly found.

A slur can be added to the initial strike of the G note by the index finger.

Track 98

In addition, the thumb can add an extra note to the slur.

Track 99

The bottom and top positions for this scale can also be combined to make this common phrase.

Track 100

Also, the entire scale can be worked up and down, while repeatedly playing the root on top with the fifth finger.

Track 101

Or you can do something slightly cooler by combining several things covered so far.

Track 102

Repeating a chord in the left hand while going up and down the scale in octaves with the right hand is another well-known way to employ a blues scale, either major or minor. This technique usually requires a rhythm section, so that you have a bass line going on and a drummer keeping the backbeat. What you play might sound something like the example that follows. Notice how the left-hand chord does not change from its C9 voicing.

Track 103

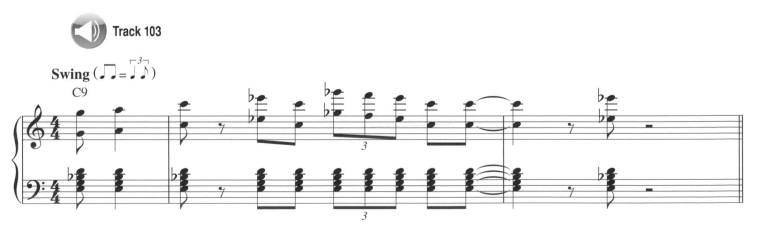

Since this scale does not require transposition when the chords change in a blues progression, either the I, IV, or V chords could be played in the left hand while the same minor blues scale is used in the right.

In the Style of...

As I mentioned earlier, Otis Span was one of the piano players to use the minor blues scale compellingly. Although his style is difficult to imitate, it's worth the time you take to study it. Spann commonly played in the keys of A, D, and E – as well as C, G, and F. The minor blues scale falls under the fingers quite nicely in A, D, and E. Furthermore, those three keys share the same shape for their minor blues scales. In other words, if you play the minor blues scale in A, then close your eyes and start on D or E and play the same A blues scale, pretending you are still in A, then it will be exactly the same shape. It will *feel* the same under your fingers. Here is the minor blues scale in A.

Track 104

Try the same shape and pattern starting on D. Then try it in E. They should all feel exactly the same under your fingers. The way you learn to use this scale in any of these three keys will be easily transferable to the other two.

Here is how Otis Spann might use this scale during a blues in the key of A.

Track 105

The preceding are ways to use the minor blues scale, but not the *only* ways. They are a jumping-off place to spur your own creativity. Use the techniques and approaches introduced here in the songs you are already playing. Give them a try. Take chances. See how they sound. If you don't like the way they sound, trust your ear and don't use them. Not every song, and not even every blues song, is appropriate for the minor blues scale. But you can learn this only by trial and error, leading to success. When I first learned how to use the blues scales, I wanted to fit them into little nooks and crannies during my solos, as fills between vocal lines – and even as transitions between chords in almost every song I knew how to play. I probably overdid it, but I learned how to use them effectively, and when *not* to use them.

CHAPTER 12
THE RIGHT WAY TO PLAY BOOGIE WOOGIE

Boogie woogie centers on dance. Think of a modern DJ filling a club with music for dancing and mingling. That was the task of the early boogie woogie players, traveling from town to town by railway and stopping wherever there was a barrelhouse with a piano. The pianist's job was to create a lively environment for people to dance.

"Does this make me want to dance?" That's the yardstick by which you should measure whether you are playing this music correctly. If you are not the dancing type, then look at your audience while you are playing. Are they tapping their feet? If I am performing and I look out and see my audience just sitting there, not moving any part of their bodies, then I know something is wrong. I take a second to step back and assess what I am doing. Is the tempo unsteady? Am I playing too many licks with the right hand and not concentrating on keeping the groove? Am I just blasting everything and not playing with interesting dynamics? Usually this reality check helps me get back in the groove to make people start moving.

Make no mistake about it, boogie woogie is the easiest music in the world to play *poorly*. To play something in the groove, no matter what style, is one of the hardest things. There are many pitfalls and distractions that can take your concentration off playing in the groove; in fact, one hardly hears music played in a solid groove anymore. Everyone "talks the talk," but few "walk the walk." However, when a solid groove is established and maintained, it's a magical experience. It creates an energy that is self-sustaining, uplifting, and energizing – a breath of fresh air. Furthermore, it compels all who hear it to start moving.

There are a few different elements that must combine to create a groove.

Time: Having a good sense of time and maintaining a steady tempo is essential to playing a groove. If a song is speeding up and slowing down throughout, it disrupts the groove. Consistency of time is of paramount importance. The more solid your tempo, the easier it will be for you to establish a groove. This is not only the job of the left hand, but everything you play must be in time and in the groove.

Chops: When someone says a musician has "chops," they mean the person has strong technical skills. Having good technique on your instrument and being able to employ it readily in performance is having good chops. This doesn't mean being able to play a million notes. In fact, that is one of the pitfalls of up-and-coming players. They play too much. And all those notes get in the way of the groove. Just play what needs to be played, and do it well.

Simplicity: A good groove is rarely, if ever, complicated. Remember, the point is to make people *dance*. If that is your focus, you will naturally gravitate toward simple and repetitive phrases and ideas. Playing a million notes may have its time and place in the course of an evening's performance, but remind yourself that less is more.

Dynamics: This is the subtlest element of establishing a groove, and the one that is most regularly overlooked. In a way, dynamics need to be happening on the macro and micro levels of every song. Let's take a closer look at this now.

Overall Dynamics

Chances are, many of the bands you hear live are not using dynamics effectively. They start a song at one volume and stay at the same volume until the song ends. By bringing dynamics – increases or decreases in volume – to a song, an entirely new depth of emotional meaning is added. It's like including a third dimension to an otherwise two-dimensional picture. It also has a profound effect on the audience. Think about it: When something is uncomfortably loud, the natural tendency is to back *away* from the noise or at least brace yourself against it. When something is almost inaudible and you are interested in hearing what is going on, the natural tendency is to lean in *toward* the sound to get a better listen.

If the overall volume of a performance is comfortable, where the listener is not backing away or straining to hear, then we say the performer has "room to go somewhere." He can get louder or softer temporarily and thus have control over his audience's attention without causing them too much discomfort. A balance between comfort and discomfort is what makes for an interesting and dramatic performance and dynamics play a crucial part in pulling it off.

The best boogie woogie and blues musicians know this well, and use it to their advantage. What we call a "break" in boogie woogie is one example. A break is usually a four-measure section on the I chord where the left-hand bass pattern is suspended. When the bass comes back in on the IV chord, the music is revitalized by the contrast.

Left-Hand Dynamics

Dynamics are essential to playing a groove. In fact, a groove is dependent on them. In each measure, there needs to be a combination of loud and soft beats. If this combination is repeated for an extended period of time, we call it a *groove*. The most common beats to accent in boogie woogie and blues music are beats 2 and 4, which make up the "backbeats."

Since a boogie woogie player has the rhythm section in his left hand, he is able to decide which beats he wants to accent in his bass pattern. Playing the backbeat is not a bad place to start. Accenting beats 2 and 4 means you must not only make them louder, but all the other beats need to be *softer* as well. Practice it with this left-hand pattern. The accents are marked.

Track 106

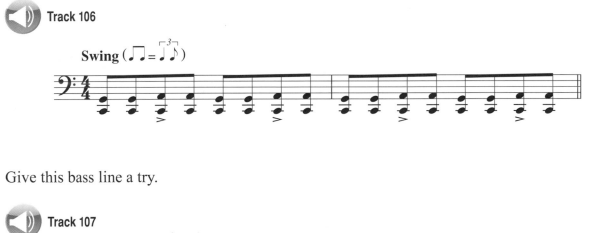

Give this bass line a try.

Track 107

You can put the accent on beat 1 of each measure, as Amos Milburn does on "Down the Road Apiece."

Track 108

The accent sometimes occurs on beats 1 and 3. Along with beats 2 and 4, these are the most oft-used places for the groove accents, but you'll want to experiment with accenting other beats as well. You might discover something cool that no one has done before. Be consistent with your accents; that's the most important thing. Some players can manage a groovy left-hand pattern by itself, but as soon as the right hand comes in, they lose focus on the left hand and concentrate only on the right hand. As a result, the left-hand groove falls apart and the song is no longer compelling. It is better to put the priority of one's attention on playing the left-hand groove rather than focusing so much on the right hand. This sounds counterintuitive, but it is better because then the right hand wants to play things that are phrased more in sync with the left hand. When this happens, you are playing in the groove with *both* hands, which is the ultimate goal.

Establishing and maintaining a groove is the *most* important thing when playing boogie woogie. Now that you have gotten some of the bass lines and right-hand licks under your fingers, make this the focus of your practice. *Always!* Playing with a groove that makes people want to get up and dance is the essence of boogie woogie.

Metronome

Practicing with the metronome is a *must*. If you don't have one by now, stop reading this page immediately and go buy one.

There are two helpful ways to use a metronome. The first is to adjust it to the desired speed of the quarter note, and then play along. I recommend this way first, until you get the hang of it. Start with the metronome and just a left-hand pattern of your choosing. Stay in the same key until you can settle into a nice groove with the click. Then, still playing just the left hand, go through a 12-bar blues. Try to make smooth transitions between chords, so that there are no hiccups in the rhythm. Now add the right hand. Start simple if you like, maybe using the hand independence drill with a basic chord in the right hand. Play Lick #1 next. Gradually increase the complexity of the right-hand pattern while maintaining the steady rhythm of the left hand in alignment with the metronome.

The second way is to put the metronome click on the half note instead of the quarter note. For example, if you are playing your shuffle blues bass pattern at $\quarternote$ = 110 bpm, adjust the metronome to 55 bpm. Now the metronome will click on beats 1 and 3. However, what you want to do is place those beats on 2 and 4. Now it will sound like you are playing with a drummer who is hitting his snare drum on the backbeat. It takes a little practice to get the hang of this. Turn on your metronome and with each click say alternately, "two, four, two, four, two, four," etc.; that's one way to get started. Then fill in the spaces of silence where 1 and 3 would be by saying "three" and "one." So, your counting might sound like this, with bold indicating when the click strikes: "**Two, four,** two, **four,** two, three, **four,** one, **two,** three, **four,**" etc. Once you have the counting going, start playing with your left hand, coming in on beat 1. This is the way I practice with the metronome. It is a bit more challenging, but a lot more fun when you do.

CHAPTER 13
TURNAROUNDS, BREAKS, INTROS & ENDINGS

Aside from a steady left-hand bass pattern, there are other important aspects characteristic of boogie woogie and blues music: turnarounds, breaks, intros, and endings. Not every song has them all, but many have one or more. After learning a few, you will be able to recognize them or their variations when you hear them.

Turnarounds

Let's start with the turnaround. This is the most versatile of the four elements mentioned above, because it can also be used as an intro or ending.

The function of a *turnaround* is just as the name sounds, to turn you back around from the end of the song to the beginning again. In a 12-bar blues, the turnaround occurs during the last two bars of the form. Turnarounds are totally optional; a song either has them or it doesn't. However, they can break up the monotony of the last two measures (11 and 12) of the I chord followed by measures 1–4 of the I chord in the next chorus, which together sound like six measures of the same chord. The insertion of a turnaround can also reenergize each new chorus. Turnarounds are used not only in 12-bar blues, but 8-bar, 16-bar, and 24-bar blues as well – where they always appear in the last two measures.

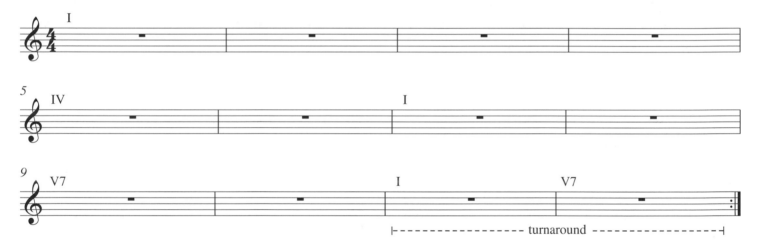

A turnaround's harmonic aim of is to go from the I chord to the V chord, which in turn leads back to the I chord at the top of the form for the next chorus. In the key of C, the left hand will walk from C up to or down to G, where it will stay for one measure. The chords in measure 11 of a 12-bar blues turnaround sort of "collapse" from a C7 on beat 1 to a C triad on beat 4 as the left hand walks.

 Track 109

Here is how we will voice it.

Track 110

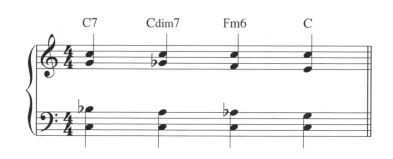

When played in context, it sounds something like the example below. You'll notice we include a C6 chord at the end, which represents measure 1 of the next chorus. This is only a placeholder for the harmonic resolution that would occur in a real context. The intention here is that you become accustomed to hearing that a turnaround is not an ending place, but a *transition* back to the top of the form. In a real context, you would begin measure 1 of the next chorus with the bass pattern of the song and whatever lick you wanted to play in the right hand.

Track 111

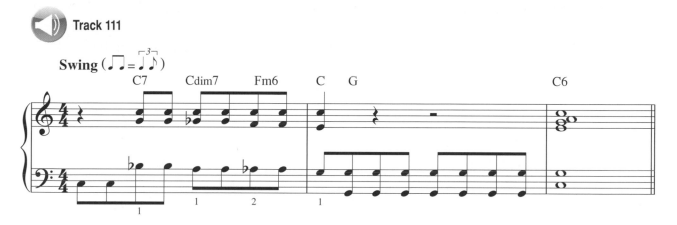

Here is a rhythmic variation of this same turnaround.

Track 112

Track 113 demonstrates a pleasing way to syncopate the turnaround and add an older, classic blues feel. Notice how the left hand is playing quarter notes instead of eighth notes, but the only difference in the underlying chords is the insertion of the #5 (Ab9) before the V chord.

Note: The audio example does not include the C6 chord resolution at the end.

Track 113

If walking *up* to the V chord, the bass line movement is C (root), E (3rd), F (4th), F♯ (#4th) and G (5th). If walking *down* to the V chord, the bass line moves C (root), Bb (b7th), A (6th), Ab (b6th), and G (5th). These melodic formulas are easy to remember; memorize them immediately. Remember Lick #3, the Yancey Lick? It can also work well as a turnaround.

Track 114

Let's see how we might incorporate a turnaround into our daily lick practice. Imagine you are practicing Lick #2 and want to play it a 12-bar blues. It might sound something like this.

Track 115

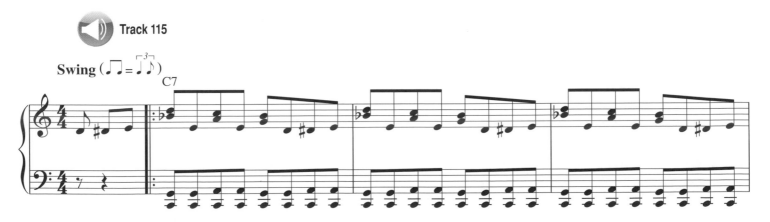

Turnarounds are so versatile they can be used as intros and endings to songs. To use a turnaround as an intro, simply start the song with it. To use a turnaround as an ending, simply resolve to the I chord in the last measure *instead* of going to the V chord. In the following example, we also create a half-step resolution before the ending chord (C9) by inserting the same chord, but raised a half step (D♭9). This is an everyday sound; you'll recognize it when you play it. Here is an example of how you might start and end a song with the same turnaround.

🔊 **Track 116**

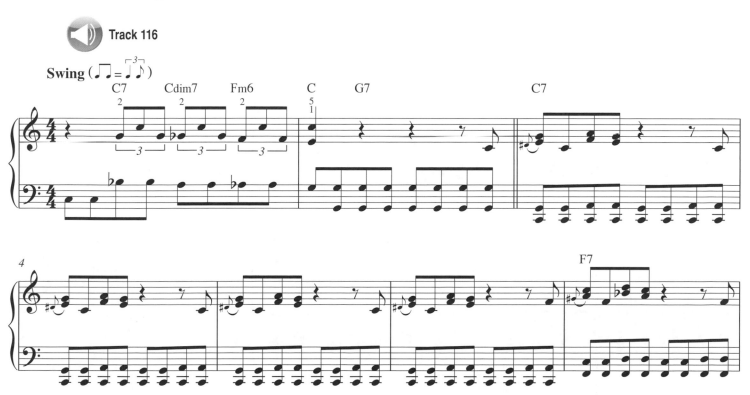

Breaks

A *break* in boogie woogie music refers to a section of the song where the rhythm is temporarily suspended, usually for four or eight measures. After the break is finished, the rhythm resumes. This technique has a revitalizing effect on the song and gives dancers a chance to be creative as well. A typical break contains the same chord structure as a full turnaround, or some combination of just the first two chords of I7 and Idim7.

Even though the rhythm is temporarily suspended, the *time* is not. The break usually takes up measures 1–4 of the form. When the rhythm resumes, it does so on the IV chord in measure 5. The remaining eight measures are played out as usual. Here are two examples of what a break might sound like. They begin with measures 9–12 of the previous chorus to demonstrate where a break is to be placed.

Track 117

Track 118

$\quad \downarrow = 195 \ (\sqcap = \overset{3}{\overbrace{\downarrow \downarrow}})$

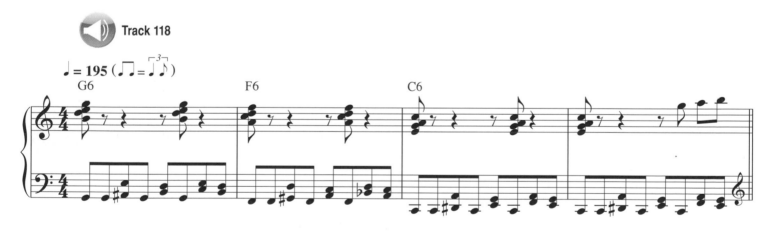

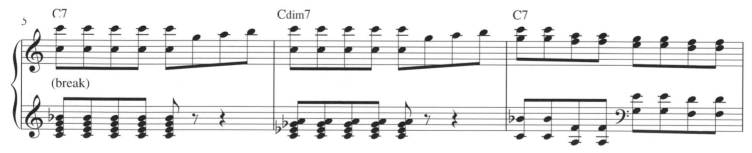

(break)

If you start the song with a break, it can also serve as the *intro*. "Boogie Woogie Dream," "Boogie Woogie Prayer," "Roll 'Em Pete," and "Meade's Blues" are all songs that start with a break. "Meade's Blues" is also an example of how the intro break may last for eight measures instead of four.

Intros

There are three common ways to start a boogie woogie song:

- With a *break*

- With the left-hand bass line alone

- With the V chord followed by the last three measures of the 12-bar form

We've already mentioned a few songs that begin with a break. "Sixth Avenue Express" by Albert Ammons and "Down the Road Apiece" by Amos Milburn are two songs that commence with just the left hand. A blues song is more likely than a boogie woogie song to start on the V chord. However, Katie Webster's "C.Q. Boogie" is an example of a boogie woogie that starts on the V chord with stop-time and sounds more contemporary. By contrast, any number of slow blues songs start on the V chord, such as "Five Long Years" by Muddy Waters, "Good Morning Mr. Blues" by Otis Spann and "Tuff Luck Blues" by Big Maceo Merriweather.

One of my favorite ways to start a slow blues from the V chord comes from Otis Spann.

Track 119

Endings

The majority of endings to blues and boogie songs share one common feature: the rhythm. The notes are somewhat incidental, as long as that recognizable *rythm* is heard. This next musical figure is the rhythmic notation of a blues *ending*. No notes, just the rhythm. Tap it out on your knee. Chances are you will recognize it.

It is amazing how universal this rhythmic figure has become. Any musician who is familiar with blues music knows it, and it is the go-to way to end a song at a jam session. Even if someone in the band hasn't heard the song before, as soon as he hears this rhythm starting to be played, he knows that it's time to end the tune.

On piano, this rhythm is usually played in the left hand in one of two ways, as shown in Tracks 120 and 121.

Track 120

On top of these left-hand figures, the right hand can play almost any lick, provided it begins on the "and" of beat 1. This is important. The *downbeat* of the ending rhythm must be reserved for the bass note only.

Let's play an ending by incorporating Lick #1 in the right hand. Here, the ending chord (C9) is played on the second eighth note of beat 2. The half-step slide down to the final chord of the song, Db9 to C9 in this example, is a stock-in-trade technique. It's worth practicing in any key you play blues. Its timing usually occurs exactly as you see written here.

Track 122

You can also play a combination of licks during the ending rhythm/bass line. In this example, the ending chord occurs on beat 4, which is also ubiquitous.

Track 123

Experiment with putting different licks of your choosing over the standard "ending rhythm."

CHAPTER 14
HOW TO PLAY BY EAR

When I first began learning how to play boogie woogie as a child, my teacher would show me a left-hand pattern and a right-hand lick and then demonstrate how they went together. I would record it on my little tape recorder and go home and try to imitate the recording I'd made. I guess this is what people call "playing by ear." I thought it was normal. I had taken lessons for about six months prior to starting blues piano lessons. That had required learning melodies and notes from sheet music. I was never much good at that. Learning to play by watching and imitating was much more fun. As I got older, I eventually learned how to read music better, but even now when I have to learn a new song, listening to the recording and copying the way it sounds is *much* faster than my reading abilities. And what's more, when I learn things by listening, they make sense. They are easier to remember because I'm mapping out the chords, the bass lines, the licks, everything in my head as I *listen*. Listening, after all, is what music is all about. And that leads us to the first step in learning to play by ear.

When learning something from a recording, be prepared to stop and replay small segments of the recording many times. My friend and master boogie woogie pianist Bob Seeley said that – when he was learning songs in his youth – he replayed certain parts of records so much he wore them out!

How to Listen

When you begin to play by ear, you must learn how to dissect a song while listening to it. Don't just play it on your device and sing along with the lyrics. There are many things to listen for if you intend to learn it. What key is it in? What is the bass line? What are the chord changes? Is there a bridge or "B section"? What exactly is the pianist playing? I can tell all these things just by listening to a song one time, as long as I know what key it is in. I don't even have to be seated at a piano. This isn't a magic talent I was born with; it's a skill I developed over time by figuring out song after song after song… for 25 years. We're going to assume you are a beginner to this and lead you through the step-by-step process I used to go through while sitting at the piano.

Know the Key

Discovering the key is the first step in figuring out a song from a recording. What is the I chord? If it's a 12-bar blues, what are the IV and V chords?

To do this, you must be able to match pitches. If your friend sings or plays a given note on another instrument, you need to be able to plunk around on the piano and find that exact note. You can also sing and sustain a random note on your own and try to find it on the piano. The more you do this, the better you'll get. Is the note you play on the piano higher or lower than the note you are trying to find? Being able to hear that will greatly reduce the amount of time you spend fishing for the right note. Treat it as a game and don't become discouraged. If you start getting frustrated, stop the exercise and resume the next day. Learning new skills takes time, so if you find you're not making progress on something no matter how hard you try, come back to it the next day.

When you try to figure out what key a song is in, *you must listen to the bass*. If there is just a piano player, zero in on his left hand and the lowest note you can hear. If there is a bass player, listen to them. You don't need to copy the bass line right away; just find the root (tonic) of the chord that occurs in the bass line over and over.

When figuring out what key a blues song is in, start the song from the beginning. It's fairly safe to assume the song will start on the I chord, or at least it will after the intro. If the I chord is played for four measures, you have four measures to hit every note in the bass register until you find one that seems to match. Start the song from the beginning time and time again until you find it.

Like a lot of popular music, most blues and boogie woogie songs begin on the I chord, but not all. However, virtually all end on the I chord.

Once you have found what you believe to be the I chord, pause the recording and figure out what the IV and V chords should be. Now start the recording again, playing the bass note you have chosen on every quarter note, regardless of what is going on in the recording. Place your bass notes somewhere in the two octaves below middle C. After four measures, play what you believe is the root of the IV chord and so on. If it sounds like you have the right root notes, you probably do. Trust your ear.

Discovering the key of a song is probably the hardest step. If it comes easy to you, congratulations! If not, don't stress about it. Keep trying and you will learn how to do it. Seek out someone who knows how to do this; ask them to help you a couple of times until you can do it on your own. You might also look at the sheet music or check online to see what key the song is in. Don't get hung up on this step. If there is a song you want to figure out or play along with and you can't use your own ear to find the key, use another resource to determine the key of the song and move forward. In the meantime, keep trying to match pitches until your skills improve.

Know the Changes

Now that you know the key or at least the I chord, sit back and just listen to the song. Can you tell *when* the chord changes? Chances are, you have an intuition about it and you can tell. Now, count the measures between the changes. If you have trouble counting measures, consider asking a friend who is a musician for help, or take a lesson from a music teacher.

Some well-known and celebrated blues musicians – like the legendary B.B. King – had trouble counting measures when they first began playing professionally. They needed help from their more experienced bandmates.

Does the timing fit the changes of a 12-bar blues? Draw a chart of the song on a piece of paper, using little rectangles to represent measures. Indicate on your chart where the song changes chords. If it looks like a 12-bar blues, try checking your bass notes as described above.

If the song doesn't seem like a 12-bar blues, count how many measures are in the form before it repeats. Knowing *when* the chords change is prerequisite to knowing *what* the changes are.

Luckily, in most blues and boogie woogie songs there are only three possible chords: I, IV, and V. When you figure out the I chord, you will know the other two. Occasionally, there are other additional chords, like the II, III, VI, #IV diminished, and #V chords. But once you get more familiar with different forms of the blues and figure out a few songs, these won't throw you for a loop.

Figure Out the Piano Player's Licks

This is the fun part! Once you know the key of the song and the chord changes, the next step is to figure out *what* is being played. Your success in this arena depends largely on your familiarity with the "eight licks" approach. This is exciting, because almost everything you hear in a boogie woogie piano piece has already been presented in this book in some form. The thrilling thing now is to begin to *recognize* that you already know how to play what you are hearing.

Let's say you want to learn how to play "Yancey Special" by Jimmy Yancey. Find a version online and listen to it. See if you can find the version re-released on the album *Chicago Piano, Volume 1.* How does it start? With just the left hand, right? When does he go to the IV chord? I'll give you a hint: It is a 12-bar blues!

Now plunk around in the bass register until you figure out the key. (The answer is at the end of this section.) So, you know the key and the 12-bar blues form. What is the bass pattern he is using? Do you recognize it from Chapter 2? Turn back to those pages and see if you can find it. Now start the song again and play along with the recording, using the appropriate bass pattern. Stop reading here and accompany the master Jimmy Yancey for a few choruses.

Now it's time to listen to the right hand. Start the recording again from the beginning and play along. What chord are you on when Jimmy's right hand comes in? You should be on the I chord, just about to go to the V chord.

Let's not worry about what his right hand is doing when it comes in. Instead, let's skip to the beginning of the second 12-bar chorus. Does this lick sound familiar to you? It is a variation of Lick #3, the "Yancey Lick." (*Of course!*) Try to manipulate Lick #3 to sound more similar to what Jimmy Yancey is playing. Don't worry about what he is doing over the last six bars of the chorus yet, just concentrate on measures 1–6. Take as much time as you want here. When you are ready, read on.

Now on to the next chorus. There are a lot of repeated single notes. Can you figure out what they are? They outline a regular old C triad in first inversion (E-G-C). Play around with these notes until you figure out the pattern. Then, before going to the IV chord, Yancey ascends the notes of the C major blues scale with an added ♭7th on top. Over the IV chord it's back to the "Yancey Lick."

The fourth chorus is again the "Yancey Lick," except this time played in 3rds instead of 6ths.

By now, you have probably started to notice that the last six bars of each chorus are the same. Here's a hint to help you figure out what Yancey is doing. He is playing a combination of things based on Lick #3 and Lick #4. See how far you can get. Since the last six bars of this song are pretty much always the same, once you determine what he is doing, you have half the song figured out!

Note: "Yancey Special" is in C.

Listen for the Top Note

Whenever I'm trying to figure out something new and it's stumping me, I listen for the top note of the phrase. This is the easiest to hear. If I already know the bass note and the chord at that particular place, it helps me determine how to fill in the rest of the chord or line underneath that top note. Use your reason, knowledge of music theory, and whatever other resources you have at your disposal to complement the work you are doing with your ears.

Close Enough Is Good Enough

One thing to remember when learning boogie woogie and blues songs by ear: It should *not* be an exact science. People who play boogie woogie songs note-for-note like the recording are not highly regarded by other musicians. The spirit of this music is *self-expression*; even if you could figure out note-for-note what another player is doing, you are still expected to "make it your own." No one wants to hear someone who is a "record player," because we all have one of those at home. So, if you are trying to figure something out from a recording and you get it close but not exactly, be happy that you got it close and play it that way. Now it's "your way."

This is not just some philosophy I'm making up so you can feel better about yourself. It's the tradition. If you listen to Jimmy Yancey, Albert Ammons, Pete Johnson, and Meade Lux Lewis all play "Yancey Special," you are going to hear four unique versions of the song.

This tradition of making a song your own, and not playing something the same way every time, goes back a long way. In 18th-century New Orleans, the slaves had Sundays off from work. They were allowed to gather at a place now known as "Congo Square," where they would dance, sing, and play music. If someone came up with a good song or groove, they couldn't take out a mobile device and make a video recording of it as we do today. Instead, they had to remember it as best they could during the week so they could try it again next week. Inevitably, the way they had remembered the song from last week would change. So each week it was a little different. Later, when piano players were traveling in the South to play for the workers, they would sometimes run into other piano players and trade ideas. But, having no way to make a recording, over time an idea that got exchanged would evolve into something different than the original. Thus, even though two piano players might be playing the same song, they would each have their own version of it, intentionally or not.

So don't think you need to copy someone *exactly*. We want to hear *your* way of playing something. Get it close, and that's close enough. Then feel free to change it over time as you feel it.

CHAPTER 15
COMBINING THE LICKS & SOLOING

By now you are getting more familiar with the "eight licks" and are becoming able to recognize them when you hear players use them. However, people rarely play only one lick at a time. What you are hearing as *one lick* is more likely to be a combination of some of the licks you have already learned.

For example, let's take a look at "The Lick" you can do only on piano. *Everybody* has their own way of playing it, from Huey "Piano" Smith to Dr. John to Albert Ammons to Pinetop Smith. It's the opening lick of "The Rocking Pneumonia and the Boogie Woogie Flu," and the same lick Pinetop Smith plays at the end of his break choruses in "Pinetop's Boogie Woogie." If we take the "eight licks" approach, this one is a combination of Lick #1, Lick #5, and Lick #4 – in that order. If you can think about it that way, it will help you remember it in terms of hand position instead of notes. You will also be more likely to come up with your own unique method to play it.

Here is how Huey Smith played it.

Track 124

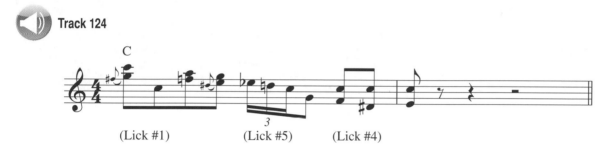

(Lick #1)   (Lick #5)   (Lick #4)

Pinetop Smith played it like this.

Track 125

(Lick #1)   (Lick #5)   (Lick #1 or Lick #3 in 3rds)

"Combination of licks" doesn't mean each lick is played note-for-note the way we've presented them. It means the basic hand position and the notes used are the same. See if you can recognize their similarities.

Here are a few sample solos to give you ideas of how you might combine the licks. There is a slow blues, a medium shuffle, and a fast boogie. The Licks don't always appear exactly as presented, but they are variations, and that's the point. If you can recognize them for their basic shapes and hand positions, you will be able to remember them more easily and recognize that you know how to play them when you hear them.

Track 126

Slow Blues

(intro from the V)

(turnaround)

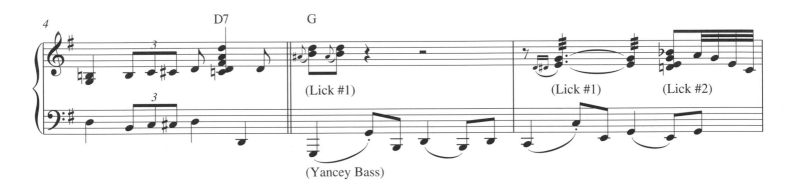

(Lick #1)

(Lick #1)

(Lick #2)

(Yancey Bass)

(Lick #2)

(Emphasize 7th before going to IV)

(Lick #2)

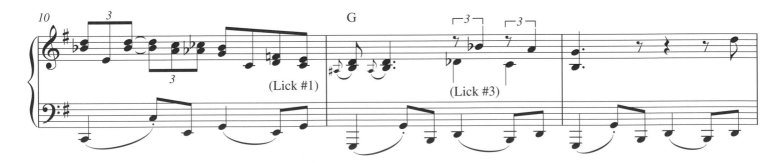

(Lick #1)

(Lick #3)

(Lick #3)

(turnaround)

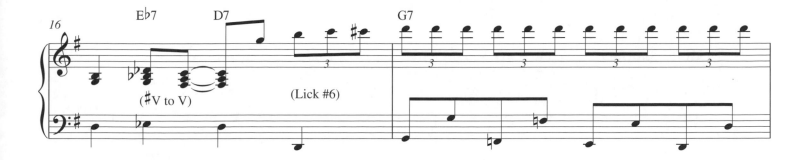

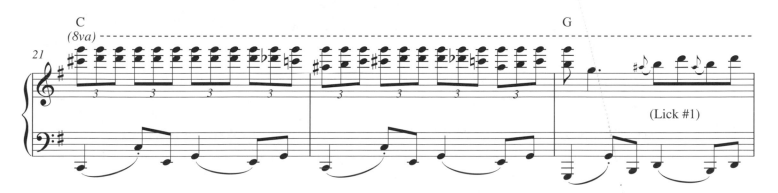

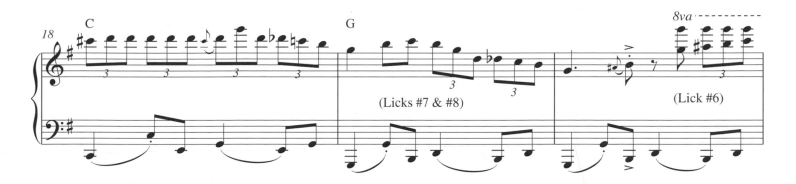

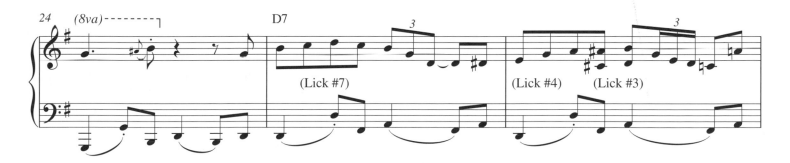

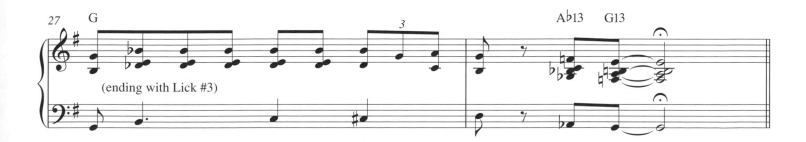

Track 127

Medium Shuffle

(Lick #4)

(Lick #3 next 4 bars)

(Lick #2)

(Lick #1)

(Lick #3)

(Lick #3)

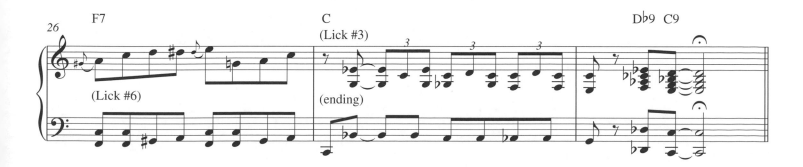

(Lick #6)

(ending)

Fast Boogie

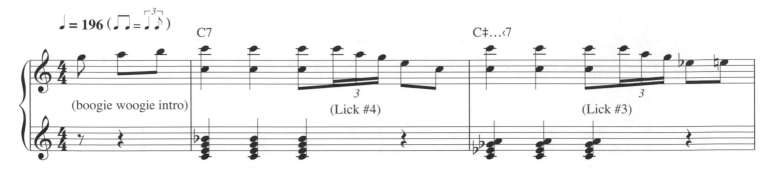

(boogie woogie intro)   (Lick #4)   (Lick #3)

(Lick #7)

(Lick #1)

(Lick #4)   (Lick #5)   (Lick #4)   (Lick #4)

(Lick #4)   (Lick #5)

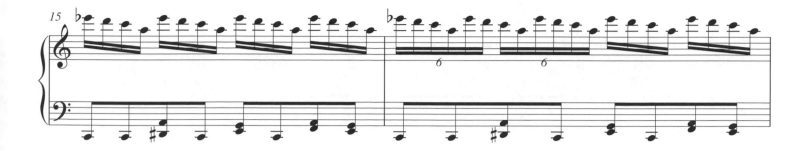

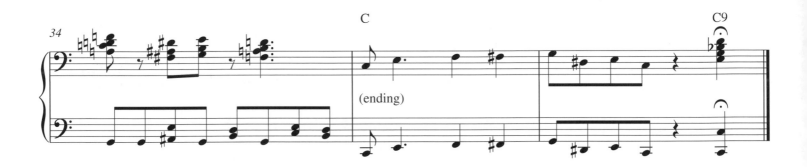

CHAPTER 16
ADAPTING A BLUES SONG TO THE BOOGIE WOOGIE STYLE

"The St. Louis Blues"

W.C. Handy published his original composition "The St. Louis Blues" in 1914. It was and still is considered a blues song, but it contains many non-blues elements, including a section with a tango rhythm that was in style at the time. The original song has six unique sections, but most pianists today play only two of the six. Search out W.C. Handy's recording of this song and take a listen. It's something like an up-tempo march, but we're going to play it as a boogie woogie.

What does it mean to play a tune *as* a boogie? You can do it to almost any song. "Happy Birthday" played as a boogie woogie is a great crowd pleaser. Simply adapt the right hand melody to fit with an "eight-to-the-bar" left-hand bass pattern. Let's take only the two most popular sections of "The St. Louis Blues" and put a boogie left-hand pattern to them. The first section is in G minor and has only two chords, Gm (i) and D7 (V7). The second section is a 12-bar blues in G.

We're going to draw from Earl "Fatha" Hines and Bob Seeley for the left-hand pattern over the G minor section, and use a typical walking-bass pattern for the G major blues section.

Here is the left-hand part for G minor section.

🔊 **Track 129**

Here is the "The St. Louis Blues" as a boogie woogie.

 Track 130

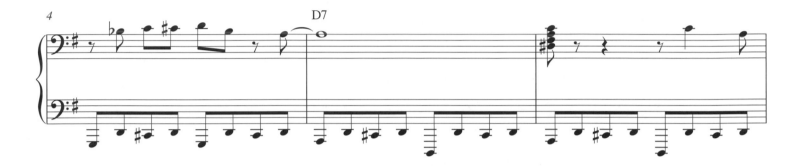

(turnaround to 12-bar blues in G)

(Fast IV and walk back down to I chord)

(Lick #1)

(melody with embelishments)

(Lick #4)

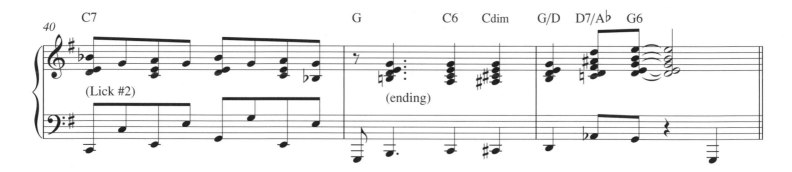

Notice how the left hand plays the transition from the G minor section to the G major blues section. It's a II–V–I progression from A to D to G.

CHAPTER 17
FURTHER STUDY

Scales and Finger Exercises

Practicing major scales wasn't a serious part of my piano study until I was about 18 years old, after I had already been playing professionally for five years. When I was 16, I ran into New Orleans pianist Henry Butler at a festival we were both playing in Cincinnati. He showed me how to practice the major scales and strongly recommended that I start doing so. I practiced for a few months but eventually dropped it. When I saw him again two years later, he asked me to play some major scales and then kicked my butt so hard I have been practicing them ever since! As soon as I incorporated major scales as a serious part of my daily practice regimen, I immediately noticed the benefits of an increased familiarity with the different keys and the geography of the keyboard – and a stronger command of my fingers.

The Hanon Exercises

When I was about 25, I met a fellow who had been a student of Vladimir Horowitz, that greatest of all classical pianists. He further helped me train my hands to relax while I play, by means of the exercises developed by the 19th-century French pianist and teacher Charles-Louis Hanon.

Therefore, I recommend to all my students who want to be good not only at boogie woogie, but also develop a mastery of the piano, that they practice all 12 major scales and accompanying minor scales and purchase the book *Hanon: The Virtuoso Pianist in 60 Exercises*. It contains all the major and minor scales and is inexpensive, under $10. It's one of the best additions you can make to your music library.

Learning the scales and the exercises is not enough. What counts is the *way* you practice them. You want to train your hands not only to know the different keys, but also to be under your command. In other words, they don't do anything without you telling them to. Their default action is to relax. Learning to relax while you play will make a huge difference in your playing. It will enable you to play for longer periods and save you from a lot of the stress and tension problems that piano players run into, such as carpal tunnel syndrome. Boogie woogie piano is no joke. It's similar to an athletic event, taking strength and endurance to play. Unnecessary muscle tension in your hands and arms will only hurt you.

How I Practice

There are five techniques you want to develop while working through your scales and exercises. If you are completely new to these things, apply them first to the Hanon exercises for a while and then the scales later.

These techniques require that you start at an *extremely* slow tempo. You are trying to retrain your nervous system… consciously. Don't be in a hurry.

Play and relax: When you play a note on the piano, the hammer will strike the string and then retract. There is nothing more you can do to the sound except let it decay or stop it. So, why keep pushing so hard? Whether you strike the key strongly or softly, afterward is the same. *Relax.* Play a note on the piano and experiment with how little strength it takes to hold that key down. You should be using the minimum amount of force. Anything more than that is a waste of energy. When you play your Hanon exercises, ignore the suggested tempo markings and set your metronome to 50 bpm. You are not going to be playing 16th notes as they are written. You are going to be playing *quarter* notes. This is extremely slow, but it gives you time to train your hands to relax between notes.

Play with the click: Your metronome is set at 50 bpm and you are concentrating on relaxing; don't lose track of the click. All your relaxing won't do much good if you can't stay in time. If you have to, subdivide mentally or aloud to stay in time; count a subdivision like eighth notes or 16th notes between the clicks.

Hear only one note: Assuming you are playing the same note in both hands, an octave apart, your hands must be playing exactly at the same time, with the click, so that you do not hear two separate notes.

Make each note the same volume: Whatever dynamic level you choose – and you should practice playing loud and soft – maintain that volume for the duration of the exercise. The goal is to play an even line, rather than having notes jump out or disappear here and there.

Make your crossovers/pass-unders as facile as possible: When playing scales, you will have to cross fingers over and pass your thumb under. Make these transitions quickly and wait over the next note until it's time to play. You should avoid arriving at the note just in time to play it.

As you become familiar with the Hanon exercises and these techniques, gradually increase the tempo. However, keep in mind that speed is not the main goal. I still, after over ten years of practicing like this, start every practice session with a very slow tempo, going through several Hanon exercises. This helps me calibrate my hands and get them in tune with my brain and ready to play.

As you learn more major scales – and, eventually, the minor scales – play your Hanon exercises in different keys, keeping the same fingering. Each day choose one or two keys you want to play your exercises in.

Rhythm Accents

New Orleans pianist Henry Butler showed me how to add rhythmic accents to my major scale practice. For instance, if you are playing the C major scale in eighth notes, you can add an accent on every downbeat, counting "**one** two **one** two **one** two **one** two" and so on. Then you can accent every upbeat, like "one **two** one **two** one **two** one **two**." Then accent every third beat, still playing in an eighth-note rhythm. Next, accent every fourth beat, then fifth, sixth, and finally seventh. By training your fingers to bring out certain beats louder than others, you will have greater control over your fingers and will start to hear different rhythmic groupings more easily. When you are making a single note louder than the others, don't forget to make the other non-accented notes *softer.*

CHAPTER 18
SUGGESTED LISTENING

"I heard the news: there's good rockin' tonight!"

–Roy Brown

There is duplication between some of the anthologies listed below, but all are worthwhile.

Boogie Woogie Blues	(Biograph)
Boogie Woogie Giants	(Jazz Hour)
Boogie Woogie Boys	(Magpie Records)
The Boogie Woogie Man	Albert Ammons (ASV Living Era)
King of Boogie	Pete Johnson (Milan Records)
The Chronological Classics, 1927-1939	Meade Lux Lewis (Classics)
Complete Recordings, Vol. 1	Jimmy Yancey (Document Records)
Cow Cow Davenport, Vol. 1	(Document Records)
A Portrait of Boogie Woogie Piano	(import)
Boogie Woogie & Barrelhouse Piano	(Document Records)
Rockin' Pneumonia and the Boogie Woogie Flu	Huey "Piano" Smith (Jax 501)
A, B, C & D of Boogie Woogie	(Eagle Records)
Swamp Queen Boogie	Katie Webster (Alligator Records)
Queen of the Boogie and More	Hadda Brooks (Ace Records)
Atlantic Blues Piano	(Atlantic Records)
The King of Chicago Blues Piano	Big Maceo Merriweather (Arhoolie Productions)
King of the New Orleans Keyboard	James Booker (JSP Records)
Crawfish Fiesta	Professor Longhair (Alligator Records)
Boogie Woogie & Barrelhouse Piano, Vol. 1 &2	(Document Records)
The Complete Candid Otis Spann/Lightnin' Hopkins Sessions	Otis Spann

ACKNOWLEDGMENTS

I would like to acknowledge those who have directly inspired and encouraged me in my own journey and pursuit of music and the piano: Ginny Snow, Judy Luis-Watson, Ann Rabson, Mark Braun, Henry Butler, Phil Kravits, Rob Boone, Daryl Davis, Bob Baldori, my *Blues Week* family, and of course my lovely Mom and family. Also a big thank you to Dave Rubin, without whom this book would not have been possible!

—Arthur Migliazza

ABOUT THE AUTHOR

Playing boogie woogie piano music is by definition a muscular vocation requiring tremendous stamina, along with great drive and unflagging energy. Many of the giants of the genre in the 1930s and 1940s were men of imposing stature with the requisite physical gifts. Figuratively standing head and shoulders above the select group of contemporary practitioners of the demanding art, however, is award-winning blues and boogie pianist **Arthur Migliazza**. Possessing unexcelled power, grace, and imagination, he is the living embodiment of the highest standards established by his esteemed musical predecessors.

Arthur began playing the piano professionally at age 13. Through his love of blues music and his dedication to the piano, he came under the wing of such mentors/teachers as Henry Butler, Ann Rabson, and Mr. B – all of whom recognized his exceptional talent.

He has been inducted into the Arizona Blues Hall of Fame and was a finalist at the 2010 and 2014 International Blues Challenge in Memphis, TN. In his 20+ years of performing, he has been privileged to play on some of the world's greatest stages, including Tchaikovsky Hall in Moscow as part of the sold-out Kings of Boogie Tour in 2013, the Glenn Gould Studio in Toronto, and Benaroya Hall in Seattle. In addition, he has also appeared on National Public Radio in the U.S. and has been a featured performer at countless boogie woogie festivals both in North America and in Europe.

In 2005, Arthur was awarded the TAMMY Award for Best Keyboardist in Tucson, AZ and in 2014 he received the Best of the Blues Award for Best Keyboardist in Washington State. His latest album, *Laying It Down*, which features him singing and playing a selection of covers and original blues and boogie woogie songs, resided at No. 1 on the Roots Music Report for Washington State and reached No. 20 on the national chart during the summer of 2014. It also appeared on the Entry List for the 2015 Grammy Award nominations.

In addition to being a riveting performer in concert, Arthur has been teaching blues and boogie woogie piano lessons since he was 15 years old. For the past 19 years, he has been a frequent staff member at the internationally famous Augusta Blues Week in Elkins, WV and at Centrum Blues Week in Port Townsend, WA.

–Dave Rubin

KEYBOARD STYLE SERIES

THE COMPLETE GUIDE!

These book/audio packs provide focused lessons that contain valuable how-to insight, essential playing tips, and beneficial information for all players. From comping to soloing, comprehensive treatment is given to each subject. The companion audio features many of the examples in the book performed either solo or with a full band.

BEBOP JAZZ PIANO

by John Valerio

This book provides detailed information for bebop and jazz keyboardists on: chords and voicings, harmony and chord progressions, scales and tonality, common melodic figures and patterns, comping, characteristic tunes, the styles of Bud Powell and Thelonious Monk, and more.
00290535 Book/Online Audio $18.99

BEGINNING ROCK KEYBOARD

by Mark Harrison

This comprehensive book/audio package will teach you the basic skills needed to play beginning rock keyboard. From comping to soloing, you'll learn the theory, the tools, and the techniques used by the pros. The accompanying audio demonstrates most of the music examples in the book.
00311922 Book/Online Audio $14.99

BLUES PIANO

by Mark Harrison

With this book/audio pack, you'll learn the theory, the tools, and even the tricks that the pros use to play the blues. Covers: scales and chords; left-hand patterns; walking bass; endings and turnarounds; right-hand techniques; how to solo with blues scales; crossover licks; and more.
00311007 Book/Online Audio $19.99

BOOGIE-WOOGIE PIANO

by Todd Lowry

From learning the basic chord progressions to inventing your own melodic riffs, you'll learn the theory, tools and techniques used by the genre's best practicioners.
00117067 Book/Online Audio $17.99

BRAZILIAN PIANO

by Robert Willey and Alfredo Cardim

Brazilian Piano teaches elements of some of the most appealing Brazilian musical styles: choro, samba, and bossa nova. It starts with rhythmic training to develop the fundamental groove of Brazilian music.
00311469 Book/Online Audio $19.99

CONTEMPORARY JAZZ PIANO

by Mark Harrison

From comping to soloing, you'll learn the theory, the tools, and the techniques used by the pros. The full band tracks on the audio feature the rhythm section on the left channel and the piano on the right channel, so that you can play along with the band.
00311848 Book/Online Audio $18.99

COUNTRY PIANO

by Mark Harrison

Learn the theory, the tools, and the tricks used by the pros to get that authentic country sound. This book/audio pack covers: scales and chords, walkup and walkdown patterns, comping in traditional and modern country, Nashville "fretted piano" techniques and more.
00311052 Book/Online Audio $19.99

GOSPEL PIANO

by Kurt Cowling

Discover the tools you need to play in a variety of authentic gospel styles, through a study of rhythmic devices, grooves, melodic and harmonic techniques, and formal design. The accompanying audio features over 90 tracks, including piano examples as well as the full gospel band.
00311327 Book/Online Adio $17.99

INTRO TO JAZZ PIANO

by Mark Harrison

From comping to soloing, you'll learn the theory, the tools, and the techniques used by the pros. The accompanying audio demonstrates most of the music examples in the book. The full band tracks feature the rhythm section on the left channel and the piano on the right channel, so that you can play along with the band.
00312088 Book/Online Audio $17.99

JAZZ-BLUES PIANO

by Mark Harrison

This comprehensive book will teach you the basic skills needed to play jazz-blues piano. Topics covered include: scales and chords • harmony and voicings • progressions and comping • melodies and soloing • characteristic stylings.
00311243 Book/Online Audio $17.99

JAZZ-ROCK KEYBOARD

by T. Lavitz

Learn what goes into mixing the power and drive of rock music with the artistic elements of jazz improvisation in this comprehensive book and CD package. This instructional tool delves into scales and modes, and how they can be used with various chord progressions to develop the best in soloing chops.
00290536 Book/CD Pack $17.95

LATIN JAZZ PIANO

by John Valerio

This book is divided into three sections. The first covers Afro-Cuban (Afro-Caribbean) jazz, the second section deals with Brazilian influenced jazz – Bossa Nova and Samba, and the third contains lead sheets of the tunes and instructions for the play-along audio.
00311345 Book/Online Audio $17.99

MODERN POP KEYBOARD

by Mark Harrison

From chordal comping to arpeggios and ostinatos, from grand piano to synth pads, you'll learn the theory, the tools, and the techniques used by the pros. The online audio demonstrates most of the music examples in the book.
00146596 Book/Online Audio $17.99

NEW AGE PIANO

by Todd Lowry

From melodic development to chord progressions to left-hand accompaniment patterns, you'll learn the theory, the tools and the techniques used by the pros. The accompanying 96-track CD demonstrates most of the music examples in the book.
00117322 Book/CD Pack $16.99

POST-BOP JAZZ PIANO

by John Valerio

This book/audio pack will teach you the basic skills needed to play post-bop jazz piano. Learn the theory, the tools, and the tricks used by the pros to play in the style of Bill Evans, Thelonious Monk, Herbie Hancock, McCoy Tyner, Chick Corea and others. Topics covered include: chord voicings, scales and tonality, modality, and more.
00311005 Book/Online Audio $17.99

PROGRESSIVE ROCK KEYBOARD

by Dan Maske

You'll learn how soloing techniques, form, rhythmic and metrical devices, harmony, and counterpoint all come together to make this style of rock the unique and exciting genre it is.
00311307 Book/Online Audio $19.99

R&B KEYBOARD

by Mark Harrison

From soul to funk to disco to pop, you'll learn the theory, the tools, and the tricks used by the pros with this book/audio pack. Topics covered include: scales and chords, harmony and voicings, progressions and comping, rhythmic concepts, characteristic stylings, the development of R&B, and more! Includes seven songs.
00310881 Book/Online Audio $19.99

ROCK KEYBOARD

by Scott Miller

Learn to comp or solo in any of your favorite rock styles. Listen to the audio to hear your parts fit in with the total groove of the band. Includes 99 tracks! Covers: classic rock, pop/rock, blues rock, Southern rock, hard rock, progressive rock, alternative rock and heavy metal.
00310823 Book/Online Audio $17.99

ROCK 'N' ROLL PIANO

by Andy Vinter

Take your place alongside Fats Domino, Jerry Lee Lewis, Little Richard, and other legendary players of the '50s and '60s! This book/audio pack covers: left-hand patterns; basic rock 'n' roll progressions; right-hand techniques; straight eighths vs. swing eighths; glisses, crushed notes, rolls, note clusters and more. Includes six complete tunes.
00310912 Book/Online Audio $18.99

SALSA PIANO

by Hector Martignon

From traditional Cuban music to the more modern Puerto Rican and New York styles, you'll learn the all-important rhythmic patterns of salsa and how to apply them to the piano. The book provides historical, geographical and cultural background info, and the 50+-tracks includes piano examples and a full salsa band percussion section.
00311049 Book/Online Audio $19.99

SMOOTH JAZZ PIANO

by Mark Harrison

Learn the skills you need to play smooth jazz piano – the theory, the tools, and the tricks used by the pros. Topics covered include: scales and chords; harmony and voicings; progressions and comping; rhythmic concepts; melodies and soloing; characteristic stylings; discussions on jazz evolution.
00311095 Book/Online Audio $19.99

STRIDE & SWING PIANO

by John Valerio

Learn the styles of the stride and swing piano masters, such as Scott Joplin, Jimmy Yancey, Pete Johnson, Jelly Roll Morton, James P. Johnson, Fats Waller, Teddy Wilson, and Art Tatum. This book/audio pack covers classic ragtime, early blues and boogie woogie, New Orleans jazz and more. Includes 14 songs.
00310882 Book/Online Audio $19.99

WORSHIP PIANO

by Bob Kauflin

From chord inversions to color tones, from rhythmic patterns to the Nashville Numbering System, you'll learn the tools and techniques needed to play piano or keyboard in a modern worship setting.
00311425 Book/Online Audio $17.99

HAL•LEONARD®

Prices, contents, and availability subject to change without notice.

www.halleonard.com

ALL JAZZED UP!

FROM HAL LEONARD

In this series, popular favorites receive unexpected fresh treatments. Uniquely reimagined and crafted for intermediate piano solo, these tunes have been All Jazzed Up!

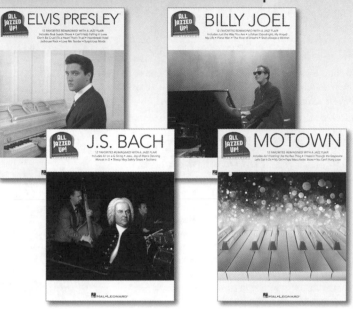

J.S. BACH
Air on the G String • Aria • Bist du bei mir (Be Thou with Me) • Gavotte • Jesu, Joy of Man's Desiring • Largo • March • Minuet in G • Musette • Sheep May Safely Graze • Siciliano • Sleepers, Awake (Wachet Auf).
00151064..$12.99

THE BEATLES
All My Loving • And I Love Her • Come Together • Eight Days a Week • Eleanor Rigby • The Fool on the Hill • Here, There and Everywhere • Lady Madonna • Lucy in the Sky with Diamonds • Michelle • While My Guitar Gently Weeps • Yesterday.
00172235..$12.99

CHRISTMAS CAROLS
Auld Lang Syne • Deck the Hall • The First Noel • Good King Wenceslas • In the Bleak Midwinter • Jingle Bells • Joy to the World • O Christmas Tree • O Come, All Ye Faithful • O Little Town of Bethlehem • Up on the Housetop • We Wish You a Merry Christmas.
00277866..$12.99

CHRISTMAS SONGS
Blue Christmas • The Christmas Song (Chestnuts Roasting on an Open Fire) • Christmas Time Is Here • Do You Hear What I Hear • Feliz Navidad • Have Yourself a Merry Little Christmas • I'll Be Home for Christmas • Merry Christmas, Darling • Silver Bells • Sleigh Ride • White Christmas • Winter Wonderland.
00236706..$12.99

COLDPLAY
Clocks • Don't Panic • Every Teardrop Is a Waterfall • Fix You • Magic • Paradise • The Scientist • A Sky Full of Stars • Speed of Sound • Trouble • Viva La Vida • Yellow.
00149026..$12.99

DISNEY
Belle • Circle of Life • Cruella De Vil • Ev'rybody Wants to Be a Cat • It's a Small World • Let It Go • Mickey Mouse March • Once upon a Dream • Part of Your World • Supercalifragilisticexpialidocious • Under the Sea • When She Loved Me.
00151072..$14.99

JIMI HENDRIX
Castles Made of Sand • Crosstown Traffic • Fire • Foxey Lady • Hey Joe • Little Wing • Manic Depression • Purple Haze • Spanish Castle Magic • The Wind Cries Mary.
00174441..$12.99

BILLY JOEL
And So It Goes • Honesty • It's Still Rock and Roll to Me • Just the Way You Are • The Longest Time • Lullabye (Goodnight, My Angel) • My Life • New York State of Mind • Piano Man • The River of Dreams • She's Always a Woman • She's Got a Way.
00149039..$12.99

MOTOWN
Ain't Nothing like the Real Thing • How Sweet It Is (To Be Loved by You) • I Can't Help Myself (Sugar Pie, Honey Bunch) • I Heard It Through the Grapevine • I Want You Back • Let's Get It On • My Girl • Never Can Say Goodbye • Overjoyed • Papa Was a Rollin' Stone • Still • You Can't Hurry Love.
00174482..$12.99

NIRVANA
About a Girl • All Apologies • Come as You Are • Dumb • Heart Shaped Box • In Bloom • Lithium • The Man Who Sold the World • On a Plain • (New Wave) Polly • Rape Me • Smells like Teen Spirit.
00149025..$12.99

OZZY OSBOURNE
Crazy Train • Dreamer • Flying High Again • Goodbye to Romance • Iron Man • Mama, I'm Coming Home • Mr. Crowley • No More Tears • Over the Mountain • Paranoid • Perry Mason • Time After Time.
00149040..$12.99

ELVIS PRESLEY
Blue Suede Shoes • Can't Help Falling in Love • Cryin' in the Chapel • Don't • Don't Be Cruel (To a Heart That's True) • Heartbreak Hotel • I Want You, I Need You, I Love You • Jailhouse Rock • Love Me Tender • Suspicious Minds • The Wonder of You • You Don't Have to Say You Love Me.
00198895..$12.99

STEVIE WONDER
As • Ebony and Ivory • For Once in My Life • I Just Called to Say I Love You • I Wish • Isn't She Lovely • My Cherie Amour • Ribbon in the Sky • Signed, Sealed, Delivered I'm Yours • Sir Duke • Superstition • You Are the Sunshine of My Life.
00149090..$12.99

HAL•LEONARD®
www.halleonard.com

Prices, contents and availability subject to change without notice.

Disney characters and artwork © Disney Enterprises, Inc.

Expand Your Jazz Piano Technique

BLUES, JAZZ & ROCK RIFFS FOR KEYBOARDS
by William T. Eveleth
Because so much of today's popular music has its roots in blues, the material included here is a vital component of jazz, rock, R&B, gospel, soul, and even pop. The author has compiled actual licks, riffs, turnaround phrases, embellishments, and basic patterns that define good piano blues and can be used as a basis for players to explore and create their own style.
00221028 Book.......................................$11.95

BOOGIE WOOGIE FOR BEGINNERS
by Frank Paparelli
This bestseller is now available with a CD of demonstration tracks! A short easy method for learning to play boogie woogie, designed for the beginner and average pianist. Includes: exercises for developing left-hand bass; 25 popular boogie woogie bass patterns; arrangements of "Down the Road a Piece" and "Answer to the Prayer" by well-known pianists; a glossary of musical terms for dynamics, tempo and style; and more.
00312559 Book/CD Pack $14.99

A CLASSICAL APPROACH TO JAZZ PIANO IMPROVISATION
by Dominic Alldis
This keyboard instruction book is designed for the person who was trained classically but wants to expand into the very exciting — yet very different — world of jazz improvisation. Author Dominic Alldis provides clear explanations and musical examples of: pentatonic improvisation; the blues; rock piano; rhythmic placement; scale theory; major, minor and pentatonic scale theory applications; and more.
00310979 Book.......................................$16.95

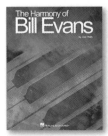

THE HARMONY OF BILL EVANS
by Jack Reilly
A compilation of articles — now revised and expanded — that originally appeared in the quarterly newsletter *Letter from Evans*, this unique folio features extensive analysis of Evans' work. Pieces examined include: B Minor Waltz • Funny Man • How Deep Is the Ocean • I Fall in Love Too Easily • I Should Care • Peri's Scope • Time Remembered • and Twelve Tone Tune.
00699405 Book.......................................$19.99

THE HARMONY OF BILL EVANS - VOLUME 2
by Jack Reilly
Reilly's second volume includes two important theory chapters, plus ten of Bill's most passionate and melodically gorgeous works. The accompanying audio CD will add to the enjoyment, understanding, and appreciation of the written examples. Songs include: For Nenette • January • Laurie • Maxine • Song for Helen • Turn Out the Stars • Very Early • Waltz for Debby • and more.
00311828 Book/CD Pack $29.99

AN INTRODUCTION TO JAZZ CHORD VOICING FOR KEYBOARD - 2ND EDITION
by Bill Boyd
This book is designed for the pianist/keyboardist with moderate technical skills and reading ability who desires to play jazz styles and learn to improvise from reading chord symbols. It is an ideal self-teaching book for keyboardists in high school and junior high jazz ensembles. Unique features of this book include chords and progressions written out in all keys, a simple fingering system which applies to all keys, and coverage of improvising and solo playing.
00854100 Book/CD Pack...............................$19.95

INTROS, ENDINGS & TURNAROUNDS FOR KEYBOARD
ESSENTIAL PHRASES FOR SWING, LATIN, JAZZ WALTZ, AND BLUES STYLES
by John Valerio
Learn the intros, endings and turnarounds that all of the pros know and use! This new keyboard instruction book by John Valerio covers swing styles, ballads, Latin tunes, jazz waltzes, blues, major and minor keys, vamps and pedal tones, and more.
00290525 Book $12.95

JAZZ ETUDE INSPIRATIONS
EIGHT PIANO ETUDES INSPIRED BY THE MASTERS
by Jeremy Siskind
Etudes in the style of legendary greats Oscar Peterson, Duke Ellington, McCoy Tyner, Jelly Roll Morton, Chick Corea, Brad Mehldau, Count Basie and Herbie Hancock will help students master some technical challenges posed by each artist's individual style. The performance notes include a biography, practice tips and a list of significant recordings. Tunes include: Count on Me • Hand Battle • Jelly Roll Me Home • Minor Tyner • Oscar's Bounce • Pineapple Woman • Repeat After Me • Tears Falling on Still Water.
00296860 Book.......................................$8.99

JAZZ PIANO
by Liam Noble
Featuring lessons, music, historical analysis and rare photos, this book/CD pack provides a complete overview of the techniques and styles popularized by 15 of the greatest jazz pianists of all time. All the best are here: from the early ragtime stylings of Ferdinand "Jelly Roll" Morton, to the modal escapades of Bill Evans, through the '70s jazz funk of Herbie Hancock. CD contains 15 full-band tracks.
00311050 Book/CD Pack $19.99

JAZZ PIANO CONCEPTS & TECHNIQUES
by John Valerio
This book provides a step-by-step approach to learning basic piano realizations of jazz and pop tunes from lead sheets. Systems for voicing chords are presented from the most elementary to the advanced along with methods for practicing each system. Both the non-jazz and the advanced jazz player will benefit from the focus on: chords, chord voicings, harmony, melody and accompaniment, and styles.
00290490 Book.......................................$18.99

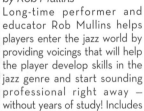

JAZZ PIANO TECHNIQUE
by John Valerio
This one-of-a-kind book applies traditional technique exercises to specific jazz piano needs. Topics include: scales (major, minor, chromatic, pentatonic, etc.), arpeggios (triads, seventh chords, upper structures), finger independence exercises (static position, held notes, Hanon exercises), and more! The audio includes 45 recorded examples.
00312059 Book/Online Audio.....................$19.99

JAZZ PIANO VOICINGS
by Rob Mullins
Long-time performer and educator Rob Mullins helps players enter the jazz world by providing voicings that will help the player develop skills in the jazz genre and start sounding professional right away — without years of study! Includes a "Numeric Voicing Chart," chord indexes in all 12 keys, info about what range of the instrument you can play chords in, and a beginning approach to bass lines.
00310914 Book.......................................$19.95

HAL•LEONARD® CORPORATION
7777 W. BLUEMOUND RD. P.O. BOX 13819 MILWAUKEE, WI 53213
www.halleonard.com

1015